13 Seats

THE WOMEN WHO DARED TO TESTIFY

13Seats

THE WOMEN WHO DARED TO TESTIFY

AUTHOR & COMPILER
Jackie E. Nugent

———————— CO-AUTHORED BY ————————

Amber Shurr-Sloss, Atisha Sanderson, Susan Stewart, Mirtha A. Coronel, Lorena Williams, Naomi C. McBean, Narkie Assimeh, Bernice Moreau, Elle Leaño, Yolando Robinson, Siobhan Bent

CONCLUSIO
HOUSE PUBLISHING

"Thirteen Seats: The Women Who Dared to Testify"
REL012130 **RELIGION** /Christian Life /Women's Issues

Printed in Canada
First Printing, 2018

ISBN 978-1-988847-05-4

Published by:
Conclusio House Publishing
Brampton, Ontario
Canada
www.conclusiohouse.com

May our collective
stories reveal facets
of God's character
not yet known to you.
May a new and renewed
faith, hope (in Christ) and love
arise within you. May
boldness and courage to
dare to share be upon you and
may you find freedom in it.

Love,
Mirtle ♡♡

Dec. 21, 2018   Seat #6

Dedication

This book is dedicated to my mother.
Mom, as you face the darkest, and perhaps the
most painful, season of your life, I want you to
know that the light of God's grace has never
shone brighter and more beautifully in you than
it does now. Even when your body seemingly
betrays you, your spirit attests to the resilience
and faithfulness of God who keeps you.
As I get older, I realize how much I am like you. I
didn't see it much before, but I see it much clearer
now, and for this I am truly thankful.
Thank you for loaning me a lifetime of your
strength in my seasons of weakness.
Thank you for your relentless dedication when
you could have quit. And thank you for your
compassion and endurance when you should have
given up on me.
Mom, I thank you for your legacy of love.
Your life is a living testimony.

Acknowledgements

Thank you to my husband Paul and family for your patience, love, and support.

I thank my firstborn son, Rishawn. Despite my flaws, your heart has always remained tender towards me. Our bond is measureless, and for this I thank God. I love you and your brothers, Xavier and Isaac, and appreciate all that you three princes have taught me about raising kings.

To my sister, Janet, who believed in my calling long before I believed, thank you for believing.

Mother Virtue, you said to me, "You must write your book before my eye closes." Beloved, your eyes may now behold the first-fruits of more to come. Thank you for charging me with urgency.

To Kerri-Ann Haye-Donawa of Conclusio House Publishing, thank you for months of loaning to me your grace, wisdom, and expertise to bring to completion the vision of this book.

To Latoy, your encouragement, especially while writing this book, has been remarkable. Through the many late and dark nights, you became the bright light at the end of the tunnel that I needed, reminding me to simply "finish."

To my beloved Embrace Women's Services family and my precious Daughters on the Rise, your encouragement and your stories of faith have inspired me. You have incited the courage I needed to share mine, too.

To my pastor, Bishop Dr. Canute Blake, and my spiritual mother, Rev. Cordell Thorpe, thank you for your spiritual covering. You have both blanketed me through the roughest storms of my life, which has equipped me with the resilience I need to testify now.

To the women who dare to testify, in this book and beyond, thank you for your courage and your obedience. You and I may never know how or when our stories may positively impact the life of another, yet we are called to plant seeds of hope in the lives of others and to water and care for them, too. The increase produced, however, belongs to the Lord, which is a sacred mystery. Therefore, it is an honour for me to rise with each of you to witness to the world.

Finally, to my Forever Friend, Jesus, thank you.

In service, Jackie.

Preface

An advertisement tacked onto a streetlight pole reads, "WITNESSES WANTED," to testify about a recent occurrence in that very place. Although you did not see the event occur, you heard about it. Gazing at the weathered invitation, you ponder whether or not you could be a suitable witness of the event. Are you credible, simply based on hearsay? Should credibility be established by a personal experience, or based on the subjective account of an eyewitness?

You may not be a lawyer or a legal representative within the judicial system, but may I propose that you just may be the witness God desires and has chosen to read and mobilize the motivation behind this book. The scenario presented is not intended to incriminate you, but rather it is a deliberate reminder of the significance and legitimacy of sharing your personal testimony. Too often, when believers should be testifying, we find ourselves hesitating or questioning the credibility of our own witness about Jesus Christ and what He has done to positively alter the course of our lives. We frequently overlook that the most powerful testimony we can give comes from our own personal stories about our encounters with Him, and instead we rely on what someone else has to say. Our truth *is* trustworthy and our testimony is *wanted*. There is a world that is in need of hearing our faith-filled stories.

This is the essence of what you will encounter throughout the pages of this book. The most powerful testimony of a life saved and changed by the love and grace of Jesus Christ comes from people just like you and me. Yes, anyone who has heard and can bear witness to an authentic experience with God should openly testify. Your voice ought not to be silenced because you *are* a credible witness.

A witness is one who will communicate and voice what he or she has experienced. In a courtroom, we are familiar with the one who bears witness or who testifies. We are also called to take a stand and testify to a troubled world about the freedom found in a relationship with the Lord Jesus Christ. There was a time when the Church adorned herself in the glory of testimonies about conversion and transformation. Sharing testimonies and stories of faith ought to be our priority, continually. Every believer is to bear witness of the Gospel's good news message. We are the evidence of God's ability to liberate humanity from sin's damaging effects on the world. Testimonies are still a vital part of this plan. When last have you shared your testimony?

In this book, you will be introduced to the stories of women who dared to bear witness and share their stories of faith and triumph. You will savour the aroma of a royal feast that has been well prepared for you. At this feast a table is set, where you will relish the comforts of a magnificent banquet and witness the tantalizing taste of rich conversations. Each author has been divinely positioned to occupy her place at the table; therefore, no two stories are the same. Each narrative, however, shares one common thread—a real, life-altering encounter with God. As you turn the pages, we invite you to dine with us by imagining the sound of each clanging glass and shiny cutlery. Hear our laughter, see our tears, and sense the converging atmosphere of transparency and safety. Each lady wears her story with a splash of courage. Her script is a graceful narrative that transposes Jesus from the pages of the Bible into the reality of her world. In her chapter, she has skillfully penned a segment of her life's story, showing who God is in her life and who He has called her to be. She shares freely from her heart with the intention to inspire and motivate anyone who will hear her truth.

At the conclusion of this book, you will find that our testimonies are a part of God's unending episode of love. Perhaps our stories will intersect with yours, although our paths may never cross face to face. As we reveal our truth, we expose lies, challenge societal status quos, and defy statistics and popular opinions, with the hope that you will bear witness to God's goodness and testify also. For this reason, this book is not merely a compilation of great messages to be shelved after reading; rather, we purpose to inspire an uninterrupted faith movement, sweeping across nations, encouraging and inviting people, everywhere, to share the impact of faith-filled table talks and testimonies.

"And they overcame him by the blood of the Lamb and by the word of their testimony" (Revelation 12:11 NKJV). We invite you now to *13 Seats: The Women Who Dared to Testify.* Pull up your chair, turn the pages, and join the conversation.

With love,

Jackie E. Nugent

Table of Contents

Foreword

Life happens to everyone, and no one is exempt from pitfalls, pains, and pressures. So how do we overcome the stuff that happens in our lives? How do we get past difficulties and move on to greater things? Revelations 12:11 says, *"They overcame him by the blood of the lamb and by the word of their testimony."* Jackie E. Nugent has brought together a group of women who all had life happen, and has brought their testimonies to life as each one shares her deep trials and her triumphant victories. The Word says, *"They overcame,"* and as you read each story, you will soon come to realize that you, too, can overcome by the words of your testimony. As we share the deep, secret places of our lives with others, an empowering gift reveals itself and a beautiful circle is formed. There is a liberation that arises because we realize we are not alone in the struggle and, like these brave women, we, too, can change our test into a testimony and help others to overcome as well.

Jackie E. Nugent is a catalyst of empowerment for women of all walks of life, with a gift for bringing great women together in an authentic and inspirational way. She is a modern day Deborah who builds bridges that deliver liberty, healing, and strength to everyone who crosses her path. Jackie is the founder of Embrace Women's Services. She holds a Bachelor's of Science Degree in Nursing, is a clinical manager and an ordained minister of the Gospel. Jackie is a true women's leader, using her God-given abilities to bring life to all who come her way. This book is her way of presenting to the world the real-life healing and reconciliation stories shared between friends over a warm cup of coffee. So sit back, get your own cup, and embark on this journey. You will experience the overcoming power of their testimonies and, perhaps, the power to revive your own testimony, too.

Reverend Tania Meikle

Co-Lead Pastor, Kingdom House Christian Centre
International Speaker
Advocate for Women through The Power of Her, World Vision Canada

Introduction

"Now David said, 'Is there still anyone who is left of the house of Saul, that I may show him kindness for Jonathan's sake?'" (2 Samuel 9:1 NKJV)

In 2 Samuel 8, King David is in his season of conquest, increasing fame, and victory. By the tenth chapter of 2 Samuel, King David's men are utterly and wrongfully humiliated by the Amorites. However, tucked in between both chapters 8 and 10 is chapter 9, which draws us to see the heart of David.

David was experiencing the abundant blessings and favour of God. Yet in the midst of a blessed season, he was cognizant of the fact that this level of increase was still not enough. To him, being a beneficiary of the blessings was insufficient without the prospect of paying it forward in a meaningful way. David desired to share his benefits with others, but not just anyone. I believe that David began to reflect on the past kindness bestowed upon him by his best friend, Jonathan. When Jonathan was alive, he was heir to the throne, yet was willing and ready to sacrifice everything for the call of God upon David's life. Jonathan was now dead, and David was forever indebted to his friend and the covenant they had made with each other (1 Samuel 18:1-4).

David was still keen to keep his part of the covenant, and asked, *"Is there still anyone who is left of the house of Saul, that I may show him kindness for Jonathan's sake?"*(2 Samuel 9:1). A former servant of the house of Saul answered and informed David that one of Jonathan's sons was still alive. Let's pause here and imagine David's reaction to this new information. Have you ever received unexpected good news? How did you react? Perhaps the king reacted in a similar way. Maybe he shouted with joy or felt somewhat nervous or overwhelmed at the future prospect. "Finally," he must have thought, "I can pay it forward." Immediately, David arranged a royal search and rescue mission to find and bring this son back to the kingdom.

The good news is, the lost son was found. However, although the son was of royal lineage, he was found living like a pauper. His name was Mephibosheth. In Hebrew, the root of Mephibosheth means "From the mouth of shame," "exterminator of shame," or "to cleave or break apart." The literal meaning of the name is either a place or instrument of destruction.[1] For the sake of ease, I will be referring to him as "Seth." Seth was found living in the house of a man named Machir, in a town called Lodebar. The word *debar* normally means "a word or thing." The prefix *lo* means "no."

---

1   http://www.abarim-publications.com/Meaning/ Mephibosheth.html#.W7IutYeWziw

Therefore, the term *Lodebar* means "no word" or "no thing." The town may have been considered an insignificant place or a "town of nonentity." This may even suggest that Lodebar was perhaps in the midst of nowhere. So how did Seth, the son of royalty, end up in such a *"Lo"* place?

When Seth was about five years old, his father, Jonathan, was killed in battle. When the nurse who cared for Seth received news of the enemy's conquest and the death of Jonathan, she ran with Seth to the royal house, frightened for their lives. Unfortunately, in her daring attempt to escape, she inadvertently dropped Seth. This resulted in him becoming crippled in both feet from that time onwards (2 Samuel 4:4).

Back in Lodebar, David's royal envoys met with Seth and invited him to eat at the king's table. A seat at the king's table had been prepared for him to restore the inheritance of his grandfather's land. This invitation was honourable, restorative, and welcoming. Seth accepted and obtained access to live as an heir of the kingdom (2 Samuel 9:13).

The pages ahead contain a parallel narrative of women who, like Seth, have found themselves either dropped, broken, overlooked, or experiencing the crippling effects of the "nowhere" land of life. Like Seth, we have experienced loss and failure, and have fallen, resulting in physical or emotional injury, often by the hands of those who were supposed to care for us. Perhaps there is a situation in your life that has caused you to feel crippled also. In this book, we acknowledge the causes and effects of our personal injuries, but we also share the invitation to hope, healing, and liberation.

The unending episode of God's kindness has also requested our presence at the King's table, where a seat has been reserved for us. Like Seth, we have a testimony to share with the world, and we believe you have one, too.

"The entire universe
is standing on
tiptoe, yearning to
see the unveiling of
God's glorious sons
and daughters!"

(Romans 8:19 TPT)

SEAT

My Journey: The Drive Home

Jackie E. Nugent

Vroooom! Vroooom! Screeech! This was the sound of Billy's Ford Mustang zooming down Everton Drive. Like a scene from a gangster movie, Billy drove away at full speed, with his foot hard-pressed on the accelerator. In the passenger seat, a young teenage girl frantically looked behind her to see if the man running with the baseball bat would catch them. The man was shouting profanities and swinging his baseball bat wildly as he chased the Mustang down the neighbourhood street. Knowing that they had just escaped, a rush of adrenalin surged through the youngster's nervous laughter. Like a fugitive on the run, the young girl thought to herself, "Free at last. Thank goodness, I am free at last." Well, so she thought. This scene would be the beginning of a life of many irrational episodes and a young girl's downward spiral of reckless and careless living.

That young life was mine.

The man chasing Billy and me with the baseball bat was my dad.

The night before this incident, I had snuck out of my parents' home to attend a reggae concert. Being an avid lover of reggae dancehall music combined with the fact that the love of my life would be escorting me meant that I had to be there, by any means necessary. At only fifteen years old, I stayed out all night. The plan was to return in the early morning, when I knew my mother would have already left for work. This way, sneaking back into the house would be simple, because I would leave the side entrance open for an easy return, right? Well, that morning as I carefully tip-toed to the side entrance and turned the knob, to my shock, the door was locked. I had been caught. My heart felt like it plummeted fifteen flights from an elevator shaft. I would have to ring the doorbell. Fearfully, I made my way to the front door. *Ding Dong.* Time felt as if it stood still as I waited for my father to open the door. Like a dog with its tail caught between its legs, I entered to face the music, but that day the DJ was not playing my song.

That morning I got a whooping that I have never forgotten. At some point during the lashing, fear began to escape and my feelings turned into anger. I felt a desire to hate my parents for being so strict with me. I wanted freedom, so I raged inside. After what seemed like forever, I heard my father utter these words, "And if you don't like it, then leave!" What he didn't realize was that his words became my license to escape. In my mind, he had just given me the permission I wanted to be free. I wasted no time calling my girlfriend's boyfriend to come break me out of this prison. After all, Billy was the only kid I knew who owned his own ride. Without haste, I gathered a couple garbage bags of clothes and waited anxiously at my bedroom window, watching for Billy to arrive.

Once his car approached my house, I stumbled down the stairs and out the front door. By the time my father realized what was happening, Billy and I were already stuffing my belongings into the back seat of his car. As soon as I jumped into the passenger seat, I yelled, "Drive!" as Daddy, grabbing his baseball bat, chased us off of the property.

Desperate times often breed desperate measures

That wouldn't be the last time I found myself on the run. That year, I was constantly on the run, evading, eluding, and avoiding the harsh realities of what was now a homeless life. My first runaway mission happened when I had an all-out brawl with my oldest sister in her apartment where she housed me. I remember the fist fight we had because, once again, I felt trapped. The freedom I had intended was being infringed upon, this time by my big sister, and I was not having it. Not from my father, and certainly not from her. Callously, I escaped to my next unknown destination.

Let me insert here the notion that a teenager on the run can be like a nomadic traveller. The danger in this type of travel, however, is that anywhere and with anyone the teenager can find refuge is usually where and with whom he or she will lodge. Sometimes that teenager will even resort to bold-face lies if necessary, in a desperate attempt to get off the street. That's exactly what I did.

I recall telling my boyfriend's mother that the reason why I wasn't at home was because my father abused me and I had to escape. I fabricated a story I knew would get her attention. I lied. Desperate times often breed desperate measures. This is a caution to parents who are kind enough to help young persons who are seemingly "homeless." Be mindful that sometimes the story shared with you may not be exactly how it happened. At the time I told the filthy lie, I had already been kicked out of a few places. And if you haven't noticed by now, you've heard very little about the love of my life. This says a lot about who was really in love with whom. I was the one in love. My boyfriend was exactly that, a boy. How could he really help me? The task of being superman was impossible for an adolescent boy to undertake. Apart from telling his mother about my homeless predicament, my nomadic expedition was a pretty independent one. I knew I wasn't his number one, and neither was I the only one. Though I was an expert in the art of escaping, I didn't love myself enough to escape from this juvenile and toxic relationship.

During this season of my life, I continued countless escape missions. I escaped the cops in stolen cars. Barely able to drive, my accomplices and I would speed along highway 401, night and day, joy-riding in any glamorous car that could be stolen, simply for amusement. I ran away from mall security guards all the time, sometimes after bum-rushing expensive boutiques of their goods to hustle and make a profit for my monthly rent fees. I remember one particular arrest after one of my escapades. The experience in custody was degrading and humiliating, yet it was still not enough to save me from my reckless, delinquent lifestyle. In fact, I continued to scam and lie my way in and out of trouble. I was still being kicked out from home to home, and friends quickly turned enemies. Fight after fight, night club after night club, drink after drink, puff after puff, I eventually became exhausted of the fugitive lifestyle.

Somehow, miserable and exasperated, I managed to stay in school. One day someone told me about something called student welfare. Being the hustler that I was, I was down for anything that would give me my next month's rent. However, what the rumours didn't tell me was that before student welfare was granted, the school's counsellor was responsible for attempting, one last time, to reconcile the student with their family. *Oh, no!* There I was, sitting in the guidance counsellor's office, mortified at the very thought of contact with my parents. There had been no communication for over a year. My world stood still as the counsellor dialled the telephone number of my parents' home. I had entered the guidance counsellor's office for a hustle, but now I felt like the one being hustled.

"Hello," the guidance counsellor said to someone on the other end of the telephone line.

"Oh, my goodness," my heartbeat felt like it was protruding out of my mouth. She began to tell the person on the line why she was calling and that I said I was no longer welcome in their home. Before long, she handed me the receiver, indicating that my father wanted to speak with me. Considering that the last time I saw or spoke with my father was at my getaway mission, over a year before, I wondered what he would say to me now.

Words can help or hurt; choose carefully

I placed the receiver to my ear and sheepishly said, "Hello?" I can vividly recall that moment as if it were yesterday. In the gentlest, kindest voice, I heard my father call me by the name he affectionately calls me, "Jack." Ever so graciously, he said it again, "Jack." Without any warning, I burst into tears like rushing water from a broken dam. All the pent-up anguish, anger, unforgiveness, and feelings of rejection and betrayal were released that instant. I cried uncontrollably as the open invitation to return home was offered to me.

Back at home, life would be better for me, right? With the support of two parents, a nice suburban house to live in, and the opportunity to better myself, I would defy the negative statistics. What more could a teenager ask for? Well, this little lady had, unfortunately, already begun a relentless cycle of pursuing love in all the wrong places. It wasn't long after returning home that I became pregnant.

Unwed and unapologetic, I was actually proud to be his "baby mamma." Teenage motherhood was not scandalous or shameful to me at all. The only problem was figuring out how to tell my parents, since they had already given me a second chance. They would kick me out for sure, and I would be back on the road, again. But this time, it wouldn't be the same. After all, I was swept away by the fantasy of starting and solidifying a new family with my "baby daddy."

After six months, in preparation for the arrival of my new baby, I finally decided to tell my parents in a hand-written letter addressed to my mother. I believe that when it's too hard to say, you should consider writing it. My letter went something like this:

Dear Mom,

I have something to share with you. It is too hard to say face to face, so I have decided to write this letter to you instead. I am pregnant. I know this is disappointing news, but I have a plan. I plan to finish high school. After high school, I will attend college and become a nurse, some day. I know you're not proud of me right now, but I hope one day you will be.

I am not sure where I will go, but I am asking you to please give me some time to find another place to live.

I am sorry to disappoint you and Daddy, once again.

Love, Jackie

That night, my mother found this letter on her pillow, but she didn't speak to me or respond to the letter for days. When she finally did speak with me, surprisingly she granted me permission to stay at home. With that said, there was no warm affection or cushy moments from her or my father. Daddy didn't even speak to me for my entire pregnancy.

Teenage pregnancy didn't cause me to become more mature, as it does for some girls; rather, it incited an even stronger desire for attention and more unhealthy behaviours. My growing belly became my symbol that I belonged to someone, even though I can't recall my baby daddy ever rubbing my belly. You know those special moments that couples share together? I have no recollection of such moments. The truth is, I was lonely and depressed, pretentiously acting as if I was happy.

My baby daddy actually came to the hospital when I was in labour. I felt like that was a privilege, yet mixed emotions emerged when my expectations were once again unmet. After twenty-three hours of labour, my baby was in distress, and I was told I had to have an emergency C-section. By that time, my baby daddy was already gone. Even with my girlfriend Dee by my side, I could feel the isolation and gloom caving in on me.

I remember still feeling sadness after the delivery of my firstborn son. Wasn't childbirth supposed to be a joyous, momentous occasion worth celebrating? The medical team had taken my baby boy away from me immediately after birth for medical reasons. This left me feeling cheated out of our bonding time. It hurt me when I came to consciousness two days later to find my baby not with me. Apparently, the distress my son experienced at birth, coupled with me going into shock and being completely drugged, forced the health team to keep my son in the nursery. I didn't hold him until two days after his birth. I remember the precise moment I first held him to feed. Once he latched, an instant bond was formed. Regardless of the pain of postoperative recovery and the stereotypical treatment I received, our mommy-baby latching moment was by far the most wonderful experience of my entire pregnancy.

Before leaving the hospital, I was interviewed by social workers who wanted me to consider adoption.

This angered me deeply. I wanted to lash out, but I understood that the system was against me, so I played along and told them exactly what I knew they wanted to hear. Cleverly, I said, "I am responsible. My son and I will reside with my parents in their large house. They will offer the additional support we need as a family." Case closed. They left us alone after that.

The years following the birth of my son were like a game of Russian roulette. I was still taking the same risky chances I had taken before, but now with a baby boy at stake. My parenting skills were questionable, and so was much of the company I kept. Pride now stood in the way of healthy love. I had become an "ABW" (Angry Black Woman) who was always on the defensive, ready for a fight. After all, I was the victim of the wreckage of an unwanted relationship, right? My fantasy family was just that, a figment of my imagination. Much like my baby daddy's identity in this chapter, the extent of his involvement in our lives remained, let's say, anonymous.

Out of brokenness, the opportunity for restoration does exist

There are many more remarkable stories that I could share about my season as a single mother, but today I reflect upon my life's confessions to illustrate that within every tale lies a life lesson. My story would merely be a mess if a message was not found and extracted from its narrative. Out of brokenness, the opportunity for restoration does exist.

In 1998, I met someone who changed my life forever. This man stopped me from running away and rid me of my escapist mentality. When I realized that I was only running away from myself, I was confronted with the part within me that was void of love and acceptance. This new man in my life gave me affirmation and significance. He freed my true identity. He helped to end my dependence on unhealthy relationships. I began to seek a true bond with the one who sought to be the lover of my soul. His name is Jesus Christ. For some of you, if you have only heard of Him, this may seem religious or even uncomfortable to hear. But I tell you the truth, I know Him personally. He is my first love, Abba Father, Daddy to my child, the One who supplied all my needs and taught me how to relentlessly pursue being the valuable woman I was divinely created to be.

I dare not glamorize single motherhood, because the struggle is real. It isn't easy, neither is it a fashionable thing. Our children are often the ones left hurt and suffering from the consequences of our parental actions. Moreover, the pain is often more than they are able or ready to express to us. Yet we often see the impact of their heartache in their grades, behaviours, attitudes, and choices. I believe that single motherhood, when viewed as a state of being rather than a social status, highlights a healthier perspective. It commands and empowers us to boldly alter and adjust the negative statistics and stereotypical labels. I am a product of this shift.

Now I live a brand new life with a brand new perspective. My definition of teenage, single motherhood was altered, because after accepting the love and teachings of Christ, I realized I was never alone. As a young, lone parent, I didn't have to use the single status anymore to solicit pity or special treatment. I no longer chose to emphasize my single social status, as if it were a syndrome or something demanding of a handout rather than the hand-up I really needed. I discovered that I actually had more control over any state or condition I found myself in than it had over me. I learned that God was always with me, enabling me to redefine my preferred future. I could confidently say that I would no longer be boxed into a downgraded, self-imposed version of motherhood. I began to elevate and honour myself as simply being a mother. Much of my thinking patterns and coping strategies had to be redefined then reprogrammed. This change began long before I married and had my other children.

Today, I am a product of grace and mercy. Through the undeserved grace of God, the statistics and stereotypes predicted for me have been defied and altered. Now free from delinquent behavioural cycles, I am an ambassador to many, including women living in shelters and those serving time in prisons. I take joy in shedding the light of hope on others who are hurting and struggling like I did. Young or mature, when identity meets purpose, the adverse statistics, stereotypes, and suggestions formed against your true identity will be defied.

In 2012, I walked onto a stage with bright spotlights shining in my eyes and an audience of onlookers cheering loudly. It would be my first time participating in a graduation ceremony. Somewhere in the crowd were my kids, my husband, and my mother. My name was being called next. This day I would receive an academic degree. And not only a degree, but as they called my name, the announcer emphasized "with honours." Gracefully, I glided across the stage. As I shook the hand of the school's chancellor, Dr. Chan, he looked directly into my eyes and said, "Well done." Despite my past failures, I was on the road to recovering the wellspring of greatness that in the past had been dormant inside of me. I graduated that day with a Bachelor's of Science Degree in Nursing, with distinction, plus a Nursing Leadership Certificate from Ryerson University.

Later that afternoon, my family and friends took photos to celebrate this incredible milestone. My mother and I posed for the final snapshot. She then took me aside and discreetly asked, "Jackie, do you remember the letter you gave me years ago?"

"What letter?" I asked.

"The one that you wrote to tell me you were pregnant," she said.

"Oh, yes," I said, quite remorsefully, drooping my head. "I remember the letter."

"Well, I still have it. I kept it all these years, and I just read it again the other day."

With eyes filled with compassion, my mother said the following words that will forever be etched in my heart, "Today I want you to know...I *am* very proud of you."

2
SEAT

Mirror, Mirror

Yolando Robinson

"**M**irror, Mirror on the wall, who is the fairest of them all?" I have grown up hearing those words in the fairytale where the princess was the most beautiful woman, and the stepmother the ugly villain. From my childhood it seemed that image was important. The many fairytales I watched and the books I read all told me that what others saw was more important than anything else. Their opinions somehow echoed through the mirror on my own wall.

It spoke to me and, perhaps, to others as well. Maybe, just maybe, the mirror has spoken to you, too. What has it said? Has it been the voice that highlights your flaws? Has it been the voice that says, without apology, "You are not enough"? Has it been the voice that shoots your ego down, time and time again? If the answer is yes, then we are kindred spirits, sisters with the same story. Only I invite you not to a pity party, for at this table, sister, we are celebrating freedom from the mirror on the wall. As a matter of fact, why don't you join me on my seat?

My hope for you is that as you sit with me on my park bench, you will find what I have found—healing by the hand of God. Here, in this space, where trees kiss the sky and the splendour of God is painted more marvellously than any water-colour painting, you, too, can be set free from low self-esteem and a messed-up self-image. You can silence every other voice that has pounded you with lies and has made a mockery of God's Word. You can stare into the mirror and claim God's truth about who you are. So come, sit with me a while. There is room on my bench for you.

By way of introduction, I want to give you a mental picture of myself. You should know whom you sit beside, as we cozy up for a journey into the past. Picture five feet, four inches of what I call curvy and evenly proportioned from head to toe. Add to this image hair that has just become fashionable, with the kinky curls blowing up the social networks and making me now trendy, with skin the colour of hot chocolate, complete with the swirls of chocolate powder not smoothed out completely, and you have me pictured pretty accurately. Still, in all of this I have failed to mention one thing: the "F" word.

This word has been the banner over my life for a very long time. It wrapped me up as a child, as a teen, as a young adult, and yes, even as a mature woman. For four decades, which embodies my entire life, this word has been my shame. It has brought me to paths I should not have gone down, as I sought to flee its rejecting power and hammering negativity in my life. This word led me into moments of depression, self-deprecation, and sin. Fat—the three letters that held so much power over me as I stared at my mirror for years on end. This word, my friend, was the punctuation to every lie told to me, and it caused me to live a life outside of God's perfect plan.

Growing up, I got used to being the bigger one amongst my peers. I outweighed my small group of friends by fifty pounds or more at any given time throughout my school life. In high school, I was dubbed "Yogi" by those whose hearts were sweet and well-intentioned. They said I was like a big teddy bear, and they loved leaning against me for comfort, literally. While they found that to be a good thing, I didn't quite see it as a good thing. I didn't want my claim to fame to be because I was fatter and, therefore, a better body to lean on. I hated being plus sized, which wasn't a description used back then. My body caused me no end of embarrassing stories, and so I can relate to anyone who feels like I did, like they don't measure up.

In my native country, Jamaica, the buses were loaded beyond maximum capacity, with as many fares as possible. It was common for the conductors to flirt, and I use that word sparingly, with women on the over-filled buses. I was around ten years old when my mom and I were travelling on one of these buses. The conductor saw me and must have made a comment that was inappropriate, considering I was only a little girl in a woman's body. My momma certainly did not keep quiet about his misplaced affections. I was not exactly pleased by her protection at the time. I did not relish having everyone know that I was just a kid in a big body. Once again, I was at the centre of attention for my size, and I hated it.

Of course, this led me on a path of destruction that led to many tears and scars that could have been avoided. The need to feel accepted overwhelmed me and drove my decisions for a very long time. I don't want it to seem as if I was unloved and unwanted. That is not my story. However, I craved being a part of the "Bold and Beautiful" club. I wanted to feel attractive, and that was something I felt had to come from a non-family member. So what did I do? I went looking for love in all the wrong places. I was searching for someone to validate me, to make me feel like I was enough for them. As you might have already surmised, that did not happen.

I remember asking someone if he thought I was beautiful. Oh, the horror of his reaction. He did not tell me I was beautiful, cute, or any such words that would have boosted my ego. In fact, his inability to affirm me told me what I felt was the truth about myself. He confirmed for me that afternoon what my mirror had always shouted out at every glance I gave it: "You are ugly." I felt the tears that burned my eyes and were only held in check by stubborn pride that refused to allow him to see how he had wounded me. I was already scarred from a previous relationship, and so this was further fuel to the fire within me. He was not the first man in my life to have rejected me based on my body. I was once in a relationship with a man I thought would one day be my husband. I had borne him a son, and I thought our conclusion would be holy matrimony, blissfully walking into the sunset until death do we part. Well, our relationship went to the morgue a lot faster than either of us did, which had me in mourning for seven years. I wouldn't say the mourning was perfect, but it was complete. He was the man that scarred me the most, perhaps because I expected so much from him. He was just a man, fallible and frail, yet in my eyes I saw him as God. I worshipped at his feet until he came tumbling down.

One night after we had our very intimate encounter, he brought me, half-dressed, before the mirror. There, clad in my unmentionables, he asked me to look at myself in the dreaded mirror. I knew what I would see, but it hurt me to know that he saw it too and was not content to ignore it. No, he was dissatisfied with my body and wanted me to see that I had gained weight from my pregnancy. Apparently, I needed to do something about it, as it was now a problem for him. To say that I was a mess is not adequate to describe what that moment did to me inside. He had used the very nemesis of my life to further wound me—the mirror on the wall. It was my undoing, and it left me weakened in mind and spirit. I entered into a darkness I didn't understand or even realize I was living in until

God shone His light on me.

I remember one of our healing sessions. He, my heavenly Father, told me I was beautiful. It was not something that I could remember being told by anyone, so it was not readily received as truth. In fact, His words were like a hammer that pounded into my consciousness, chipping away at the buildup of lies that had hardened my heart. It wasn't until He took me before the very mirror that had tested and bested me that I began to sense a change on the inside.

"Look in the mirror," He said. Friend, that was the hardest thing for me to do at that moment. It was as if He had asked me to make bread out of stone. I felt so unable to follow through, so afraid of what I would see before me—ugliness. With more tears, and sensing a love for me that was indescribable, I dared to do what I couldn't. Through Christ, I was able to do the impossible, and I looked. I really looked at myself. As I stared, He brought truth and His liberty that remains as I stand in it today.

He said, "Your daddy never told you, but I am telling you, you're beautiful." Those words broke the dam, and I wept. I can't even begin to explain the healing that took place in that moment. I often reflect on how Jesus restored Peter. Three times Peter denied Christ. Three times Jesus asked Peter, "Do you love me?" To me, every time that question was asked, it cancelled out the denial in Peter's past. That day, I felt like Jesus was erasing my past. He told me a truth I never imagined or believed about myself. His Word, which always accomplishes its set purpose, was fulfilled in me. I was free.

By now, I imagine that you have a very good impression of my life as it was before I was healed. I was a slave to the scale, to the opinions of others, and, of course, to the mirror. I was bound and dragged about for years, not once realizing that I could be free. This is why I tell my story. I want you to know that there is liberty in Jesus Christ. The best part of my life is Him. So I am no longer trying to be who I am not.

I am not the girl in the magazine. I am not the girl on TV. I am not flawless. I am not perfect. However, I am the daughter of the Lord of lords and the King of kings. I am forgiven. I am loved. I am the voice that will praise out loud because "I am fearfully and wonderfully made...and that my soul knows very well" (Psalm 139:14 NKJV).

SEAT

A Voice from the Pew

Amber Shurr-Sloss

Strong, supportive, in its place. Having been born into a Baptist, church-going family, some of my earliest memories were associated with the church pew. As the third of four children, I was always looking for attention, and I had the volume and presence to demand it. Strength is the first thing I remember being known and applauded for. I was a solid, healthy girl, not terms you actually want to be described by when you are a young female.

It's interesting that some of the things we wrestle

with in our youth can be the very things that we appreciate in ourselves when we are older. I was the closest thing that my brother had to having a brother, and he took every opportunity to encourage me to fight and be strong. It wasn't long before I could keep up with the running, biking, building, jumping, wrestling pace of my brother, who was eight years my senior. I had found my place.

Immovable, accommodating, following the rules. We always went to church. First the Baptist church, then Pentecostal, then Full Gospel, and finally settled into a non-denominational, charismatic Evangelical church. I had found another place where strength and drive were applauded. We had plenty of creative freedom, having grown up in a single-parent family. As a very energetic and bright child, I constantly required redirecting, both at home and in school. By grade six, I began to get bored with school and started using my strength to get into trouble. My mother wisely chose to home school me and my little sister the following year, and although I loved being able to do my bookwork at warp speed, I was finished by noon every day and the extra time was driving me crazy. Then we got a piano.

My mother signed me up for piano lessons. My poor teacher, I lasted one year. I just wanted to play choruses, hymns, and songs that I had written. I would spend my afternoons learning songs by ear and writing songs, forcing my family to listen when they got home in the evenings. Looking back now, I can see that the hand of God was shaping me and using this time to prepare me for the things He had called me to do. My siblings, on the other hand, still tease me about it.

Now I can see many other ways in which God used to make Himself real to me. Case in point, we had a neighbour with cable TV who had invited me to her house to watch Benny Hinn on TBN while she was at work. Between that and my hours of worship on the piano, I learned about how much God loves us and cares about the things that matter to us. I learned about the reality of God and the Holy Spirit. Experiencing God in those moments was foundational in fortifying how essential His love and His Spirit are to my world. I am so grateful for those years. "We are made of all those who have built and broken us" (Atticus).

Do you have time periods in your past that seem to have gaps and blank spots, as if your brain is saying, "It's just too much to remember the details." My teenage years were like that. I was a super-trusting, super-naive young woman in a grown-up world. That naivety seemed to place me in a position to be taken advantage of. I ended up being sexually abused by a pastor for over a year, which caused an identifiable change in my personality and the way I saw myself. I wanted to die. I prayed to die. I wrestled with believing that God had a plan and a purpose just for me. I wrestled with the shame, the guilt, the lies, and thinking that I had caused this to happen. I began to believe lies about my worth that were tough to uproot, lies like "I am not of value as a person;" "I am damaged goods;" "I am only worth what I can give;" "Who I am is not worth knowing, pursuing, or loving;" "Loving me is shameful, something to be hidden." It all got shoved under the carpet. I got caught up in working harder, doing more, proving that I still had value, while not dealing with what had really happened or with the lies that had taken root in me. These lies positioned me to marry a man whose actions only branded them deeper onto me.

Things that are solid and strong by nature seem to invite opposition, and the more foreboding the fortification, the stronger the opponent. Statistics say that one in three women will end up in an abusive relationship at some point in their lives. I truly believe that the number is higher and that domestic abuse is not just a women's issue. I cannot even imagine the shame that a man in an abusive situation faces. Abuse knows no gender but definitely has character traits.

Sometimes you don't even know the impact that another person has on you until you are away from them, and even then, you may not see it until others point it out. I spent so much time and energy walking on egg shells, trying to anticipate every reaction or action in order to get the best possible outcome. If I only loved more, did more, was less needy, more affectionate, thinner, sexier, but it was never enough. I was never enough.

I had to "pay" for everything. Little by little, fewer things were worth the price. My life got smaller and smaller. I got smaller and smaller, until I barely existed. I would go out and put on a smile, bounce around, and try to convince everyone that my life was great, but inside I had shut down. I went numb. Everything was not okay. I read voraciously, went to counselling, exhausted every avenue and resource, prayed, fasted, went to more counselling, until I ran out of options. I was living as a robot, barely going through the motions. I was no longer a participant in my own life. "The tragedy of life is not death, but what we let die inside of us while we live" (Norman Cousins). God has given each of us the power of choice. The beauty of love is being able to choose. I cannot choose healing or salvation for another person, neither can I choose for them to change. I tried to downplay it to those who had seen the abuse. I made up excuses, until I no longer believed them myself, and I avoided those who saw that, too. To dive into more detail feels like a deep abyss, a Pandora's Box that I really don't see the value in opening right now.

Experts say that the roots of abuse are ownership and entitlement, that the other person feels as though you belong to them and that they know what is best for you. This is the place where overriding your opinion, controlling your time, resources, and relationships stem from. Abuse thrives in chaos. The blame is always on you and what you did wrong or what you caused the other person to do. The abuser says things like, "I was just showing you that I was still stronger," or "I just do it because I love you so much," and if confronted, "Well, you must have done something to deserve it."

Sometimes the control can play out in the silent treatment. For me, it mostly played out in hours and hours of conversations that were more like interrogations. It was nothing for us to spend four or five hours trying to deal with something, only to walk away feeling confused and drained, wondering why I brought it up in the first place. I was the one who did or didn't do something. I was the idiot. I was literally empty of tears and emotion. The last seven years of my marriage, I had a very sore throat from throwing up repeatedly due to stress. I often found that I just subconsciously tuned out. I felt nothing, thought nothing, and had no opinion. I just shut down. Somehow, I was never enough and always too much. I grew to despise who I was.

I am far from perfect, and I have made my share of mistakes. I am not trying to play the victim here. My darling, my desire is that in telling my story I will help you to identify abuse in your own world, give voice to your pain, and remind you that you are seen and you matter. You are not alone. You are worthy of love. You are such a precious and irreplaceable treasure. You do not deserve the way that you are being treated. *"If your heart is broken, you'll find God right there; if you're kicked in the gut, he'll help you catch your breath" (Psalm 34:18 MSG).*

Just breathe.

The greatest thing in all of this is the reality of God—His love and His everyday miracles. I wish I could tell you why this happened and, very honestly, I will not say that it had to happen in order to bring about a message, for that would paint a cruel, sadistic, and untrue picture of a God who is love itself. This world is full of pain and trauma, and only a few live very long in it without being scarred. God is able to take your brokenness and make it an artwork, your scars a unique masterpiece. *"We have become His poetry, a recreated people that will fulfill the destiny He has given each of us, for we are joined to Jesus, the Anointed One. Even before we were born, God planned in advance our destiny and the good works we would do to fulfill it!"* (Ephesians 2:10 TPT).

I have had to learn to stop asking why and just focus on the how. How do I journey back to a place of wholeness? How do I put into words the beauty that I have experienced in the way that God pierced through the darkness? How do I help others with my story? You see, God, your Creator, knows exactly what speaks to you, and if you have ears and eyes open to see and hear Him, He is desperate to communicate with you. I have had total strangers walk right up to me and tell me that I am beautiful. I have had children buy me plants. I have divine relationships with people who have fought for me when there was nothing left in me to fight. God has encouraged me through movies, books, signs, social media, music, and so much more. He has positioned me to hear messages and be surrounded by men and women who cover me and protect my soul. One of the languages that speak to me the most is music, and I cannot come close to counting the times when God has used songs to convey what He wants to say to me.

Whether you directly relate to my story or whether your scars come from totally different places, God is passionately trying to communicate with you that He sees what you are fighting through, that He is with you, that you are not facing this alone, and that your scars can tell a story of how you have overcome. "Even Jesus, in His glorified body, bore the scars of what He had been through so that they could tell the story of your hope of redemption" (Christine Caine).

Lies breed in secrecy;
shame thrives in silence

I truly thought I was crazy. I thought this was the closest thing to love that I would ever experience, and that I needed to give up thinking that who I am— my dreams, my opinions, my thoughts—could ever matter. In every season of life, God has strategically positioned relationships to support you. I am certainly not telling you to go and spill your guts to anyone who will listen; however, don't let those lies percolate and grow in the secrecy of your own mind. Look for the trusted people in your world whom you can share with. We need others; we are not meant to do this alone. It is not a sign of weakness to ask for help, but rather a sign of strength. You cannot do anything about what happened to you in the past. Whether it has been at the hand of your own wrong choices or that of others, you are responsible for your future and your healing. "The pain of recovery is often greater than the pain of the initial injury, but it is ever so worth it in the long run. Embrace your healing" (Christine Caine).

I so wish that I could say that the church world was helpful in protecting and guiding me. Instead, I found that I was frequently told that I just needed to submit, to do more, and that love keeps no record of wrongs. I was accused of being rebellious and overly emotional. I grew to hate my tears, to hate that I felt so deeply and that my emotions needed expression.

When you bring your secrets to a safe place and to safe people, you break the power of shame and the lies that have propagated there. Everyone is not privy to the details of your story, but find a way to tell it, because you matter, your story matters, your story can make a difference and give hope to someone else. We need to remind others that they are not alone. My silence was telling my story just as much as my words and actions were. It left things open to interpretation and the supposition that somehow I was good enough and strong enough to be who I am today all by myself. I don't want people to believe that lie about me. I have died a thousand deaths at my own hands only to be raised back up by the power, strength, life, grace, and mercy of God. My story is one of dependence on God and the help of others. It is a testament to the glory of God, and not of man.

I don't want any woman to look at me and beat themselves up thinking that my life is so perfect and there must be something wrong with them. I don't want another woman to run to the arms of addiction or abuse because of how damaged they feel. If I want women to know the power of God on their behalf, I am going to have to tell my story so that my truth can set others free. My truth is His truth—beauty for ashes, oil of joy for mourning, a garment of praise for a spirit of heaviness.

Silence has told my story long enough. It's time for the truth.

SEAT

His Treasure
Through Grief

Narkie Assimeh

L ife changed for me on April 2, 2016. I lost the most important woman in my life, the woman who carried me for forty-one-and-a-half weeks. The woman who taught me to be passionate about all I do. The woman who taught me the importance of service to others; there was never a time when she turned her back on someone in need. The woman who taught me everything I know in the kitchen. I still remember my first cooking lesson, my first pot of rice. The magnitude of that loss shattered the world as I knew it. How could I continue on without her? How could I travel 5,541 miles and not be able to see her smiling face or hear her laugh, to not be greeted with the aroma of her cooking when I walked into the house? How would I shoulder the responsibility of planning a traditional Ghanaian funeral? And how was I going to deal with all the unknowns I knew was ahead?

In less than twenty-four hours I was on a flight to Ghana to be with my father, to begin our journey through grief intertwined with the cultural expectations of both of my parents' tribes. I think about that physical journey of 5,541 miles a lot. Before I stepped on that plane, I thought of how I was going to make the nearly twenty-four-hour trip alone with my pain, thoughts, and tears. One of the many manifestations of God's love for me occurred on that flight. On the plane, there was an empty seat between me and an older couple. The woman turned to me and said, "Are you travelling alone?"

I said, "I am, but I just want to apologize in advance because I may start sobbing from time to time. My mother passed away yesterday."

She leaned over and said, "There is no need for you to apologize." She went on to tell me that she had taken a similar trip a year earlier when her father passed away in England. Between washroom breaks and tears, we chatted for a good portion of the first leg of the journey.

God always places people and situations in our lives at the right time. It's not until you reflect that you realize that although you felt alone, He was always with you.

The moment I stepped off that plane in Ghana, I had to switch into business mode. I essentially had to place my grief, along with my emotions, in a proverbial briefcase, shove it in a closet in the back of my mind, and shut the door. From time to time, the door to that closet with the briefcase was not strong enough to hold all my feelings, and they would spill out. Every time that closet door swung open, I cried to the Lord for help. "Help me through the pain. Help mend my broken heart. Help direct me through this journey, and help me to choose the right path." There were a few of these emotional spills during the weeks of planning my mother's home-going. Each time, I would experience an emotional purge of my mind and soul that helped me to regain my focus on the task of planning a flawless funeral.

In Ghanaian culture, a funeral is the largest social event in the country. It's looked at more as a celebration of your dearly departed's life rather than a time of mourning. The first of many rituals to take place before the funeral is a one-week celebration. Realistically, this should happen within a week of your loved one's passing, but with so many family members overseas, it usually takes place between one to three weeks after the death. This celebration is not as big and extravagant as the funeral, but we are required to provide refreshments and snacks for all who attend. At this gathering, a meeting is held with the immediate family of the deceased to organize the date of the funeral and our responsibilities. In my case, the meeting consisted of my mother's family, my father's family, my father, and me. This meeting was chaired by the heads of the family on my mother's side. In some instances, the head of the family could either be an immediate relative or more of a figurehead who is a distant relative and whose sole responsibility is to ensure that rituals and customs are followed.

The first portion of the meeting felt like an interrogation. They were trying to find out information surrounding the death of my mother. Imagine sitting there as someone loosely accused your father of harming your mother, knowing full well that he would never be capable of doing such a thing. This was their attempt to provoke a negative response from either my father or me. Fortunately, before entering into the meeting, I was warned by my aunts not to show any emotion, because things may be said during the meeting that might cause me to react. All I could do was sit there, hold the rage stirring within me, and pray for God to give me strength to get through the meeting. Any sign of disrespect, whether it be a hand gesture, a sigh, or an emotional outburst, would directly affect when my mother's funeral would be held. Since the head of the family had control of when we could have our funeral, I was mindful that there had been instances where a head of family had rejected the proposed date of a funeral and held up the burial to upwards of a year after death. When they were satisfied with my father's response, our funeral date was accepted, and our responsibilities for the preparation of the funeral were handed down to my father and me. In that moment, one would expect, with all the power the heads of the family were exerting on us, that they would take on some of the financial burden, but that was not the case.

After the one-week celebration and meeting were complete, it was time to plan a funeral. In the western world, when we have to plan a funeral, our minds immediately go to a funeral home. At the funeral home, you make all the arrangements, and they are responsible for the body and for providing all the services associated with planning a funeral. You may have to go in once or twice to change or confirm things here or there, but that's it. Not in Ghana. Each item and detail had to be planned individually with a variety of vendors and businesses. Everything from buying the coffin, renting the hearse, the transporting of my mother's remains, the undertaker who would dress and lay her on the bed for viewing, even locating a person who would dig her grave was our responsibility. There was so much pressure for every element of my mother's funeral to be executed perfectly because of the fear of shame and embarrassment. It seemed that what you show in death is more important than what you show whilst you are living. Everything during the funeral is placed under a microscope. The three most important elements under a microscope in every Ghanaian funeral are the food, the funeral program, and the souvenirs. If any of those three were missing or not up to standard, your funeral was not a success, and you were deemed to have brought shame upon your family and most of all the memory of your dearly departed.

With one week to the funeral, all the planning was finally completed. All the vendors were secured, funeral programs had been printed, the souvenirs were packaged, money had been provided to my mother's family to feed everyone over the four days of the funeral, and a catering service and venue had been secured for the day of the funeral for my father's relatives and friends. There was one ritual that I had to embark on, but this one I had to complete on my own, without my father. One of the major responsibilities I had as the child of the deceased was to purchase the coffin as well as a basket of all the items that would be required to prepare my mother's body for burial. I had to present the coffin and the basket, as well as a financial token, to the heads of the family and the ladies responsible for preparing my mother's remains. First, the coffin was examined along with the financial token and a bottle of Schnapps on behalf of my father. If the token was not enough or the coffin was not to their satisfaction, the heads of family would threaten to postpone the funeral. Luckily, they were satisfied with both.

Afterwards, two old ladies opened the basket and started to take inventory of the items and examine my financial token. Given that the list provided to me previously had been followed and every item and quantity was present, I assumed there wouldn't be a problem. I was wrong. They first scrutinized the token, determining that it was not enough based on who my mother was and the fact that she had lived abroad for so many years. Then the items in the basket were also not enough. At that point, I wondered what I was going to do. Were they treating me this way because they knew I was a nurse and figured I could afford more? The reality of my situation was that I had been off from work sick, for nearly a year, because of an injury.

Fortunately, I was able to give the additional token requested, and thankfully, my aunt had set aside some extra items, just in case. So the funeral could move forward as scheduled.

Funerals in Ghana span over the entire weekend, from Friday to Sunday with the occasional Monday. So early Friday morning I made my way to the hospital mortuary to claim my mother's body. As tradition goes, I would accompany the body on the almost three-hour journey to my mother's family home. My father would leave from our home and travel to my mother's family home to receive us when we arrive with the body. Her body was taken into a room where the undertakers took care of the body. They dressed her in the traditional burial gown, and she was laid in state in the great room of her family home that had been draped from the ceiling to the walls in white cloth. My mother's body was never to be left alone all day and night; people had to remain at her bedside. Groups would sleep in shifts, but for the most part, the entire house remained awake.

At about five o'clock in the morning on Saturday, we all got dressed in our traditional attire of black with red cloth accents. The final funeral rites were performed before she was transferred into the coffin and transported to the church. My father and I were called into the room to have our final look and to say goodbye. The realization hit me then that I would never see her face again. I would never see her smile at me again. I would never sit and talk with her again. I would never hear the sound of her laughter or hear her call my name again. I would never be able to call her to remind me of what ingredient I was missing for one of her recipes. It was like the floodgates had opened, and I could finally let my sadness and pain out. I can't even remember who ushered me out of the room or how I made it down the stairs to the courtyard. Soon after the coffin was closed, it was transported to the church. We arrived at church shortly after. The service was performed, the choristers sang, the eulogy and tributes were read. After the service, I was preparing to head out to the car to head to the graveyard with my father. As I entered the courtyard of the church, I heard my great-aunt on my father's side of the family call out my name. She proceeded to ask me where I was going. I thought to myself, *"What a silly question,"* and I replied, "To the graveyard." Then she proceeded to tell me that I wasn't going anywhere, because in their tribe's custom "we," as in my father and I, could not go to the gravesite to see my mother be buried. My father would have to send a representative from the family to witness the burial. That individual would come back after the burial to tell my father and family where my mother was buried and her grave cemented. I had had enough of all the cultural restrictions and rituals that had been imposed on me throughout this process and the fear of disrespecting my culture if I did not abide by the custom. Not even realizing I was raising my voice, I told her, "I am Canadian, and where I'm from we go to the gravesite and watch as the coffin is put into the ground. I totally appreciate that you have a custom, and I understand that my father cannot go, but I'm going. No one except God can stop me!" I looked over at my dad and could see in his eyes that he wanted to go with me, but he couldn't. I walked over to him, hugged him, and went with my uncle and cousin to the graveyard. Following the interment, I met up with my father at the reception, where his side of the family was, and spent some time fellowshipping with family, friends, and sympathizers. Then we had to make our way to the family home to do the same with my mother's side of the family. Finally, on Sunday morning we attended a thanksgiving service for my mother. Following the service, we returned to my mother's family home for a small family gathering, and that concluded the funeral formalities.

During this entire process I had been very open to and accepting of all the cultural expectations that I was required to meet, without objection. There were many trials along the way, but I was doing this for my mom, like she did for her mother. Even though I found myself in an unbearable situation, I found comfort in knowing that the place she took her first breath was also where she took her last. I can remember conversations we had and her telling me how much she wanted her final resting place to be back home in Ghana. So even though I miss her dearly, and the pain of losing her will never go away, I have joy in my heart that God called her home in her country of birth. Her resting in peace and power truly outweighs my discomfort while planning her home-going.

I cannot stress enough the importance of prayer in getting you through difficult times. During the three months I spent in Ghana, I can honestly say I prayed more than I had in my entire life. The time I spent alone with God, I spent asking Him to take my pain away and to fill the enormous hole in my heart. I spent time with Him along with my father, cousin, and aunt during morning and evening devotions, asking Him to protect us and guide us through a successful funeral. I constantly called on God when the trials seemed too hard to bear or too great to fix. He was always there, comforting us through His Word, shielding us from evil, and guiding us to the solution for every issue that arose. Mary Stevenson wrote it best in her poem *Footprints in the Sand*: "My precious child, I love you and will never leave you, never, ever during your trials and testing. When you saw only one set of footprints, it was then that I carried you."

Trying to navigate through grief is not easy, even if you have a great support system. Sometimes it's a challenge for others to truly understand your loss, because they may have never experienced it themselves. The process of grief isn't meant for you to "get over it;" rather, it is meant for you to "get through it." It is very important to tap into resources that will help you through your grief process. When I returned from Ghana, I found myself crying everywhere I went, and almost everything was a trigger for my grief. A friend from church recommended a grief group she attended when she lost her mom. The group was called GriefShare, a grief recovery support group where you can find help and healing for the hurt of losing a loved one.[2] If the group setting isn't for you, there are many one-on-one grief counsellors you can meet with. Another resource I found useful was an online grief devotional. Like I mentioned in my story, my father

2   https://www.griefshare.org/

and I had daily and nightly devotions. While using my Bible app, I found a sixty-day devotional called "Grief Bites: A New Approach to Growing through Grief."[33] From day one of the devotional and the scriptures attached, it felt like God was truly speaking to us.

At many points in our lives, we all experience some form of grief, whether it be the loss of a loved one, a job, a pet, or even that favourite stuffed animal you had as a child. We all move through the process of grief uniquely and exclusively, depending on our attachment to that particular person or thing. These losses can shake the core of our being, but one constant is our faith that God will always be there. He waits on us patiently to bring our troubles to Him. He said He will never leave us or forsake us. All we need to do is trust in Him.

---

3   [3] https://griefbites.com/

SEAT

Grace Within the walls

Elle Leaño

"Be joyful in hope, patient in affliction, faithful in prayer." (Romans 12:12)

We have an omniscient, omnipresent, omnipotent God. He knows, He is, and He can. He existed before time. He transcends creation. He is an immutable God. As a human being with the propensity to change my mind and my heart on a regular basis, I did not really understand the truth about God. As a child, I had a lot of questions about the Bible that were deemed inappropriate and, at times, forbidden by the faith I was born into. As one who was born and raised Catholic and indoctrinated in the Catholic schools ran by nuns, an immutable God was a facile idea. If you sin, you go to hell, simple. Unless, of course, you adhere to the Ten Commandments, then perhaps there is hope for you. Needless to say, I knew at an early age that I was doomed to eternal fire and brimstone, until my incessant questions eventually led me to the other attributes of God—He loves me so much He gave up His only Son so that I may be saved, if only I'd believe. This may sound cliché, but I accepted Christ shortly after that revelation, and I have been born again in the Christian faith for almost twenty years.

My life with Christ has not been a road filled with roses and rainbows. Over the past twenty years, whether I served Him faithfully or not, He has always seen me through the thorns and storms of my life. And that's just it; life in the natural does not cease to exist for you once you belong to Christ. The everyday problems we encounter will still arise. However, the way we respond to the thorns and storms of life will shift. Through Him, we are able. Through Him, we are made worthy. Through him, I have been able to deal with the thorns and storms of my life. He is a personal God who responds to our choices and decisions based on His love for us. He is not merely an expression, a character in the good book, or an unattainable deity. He responds in mercy and in love.

When I read the Book of Numbers, I am reminded of how much we are like the Israelites of that time. We lose focus, we lose our vision, we become influenced by the culture around us, and, sometimes, we wander away unknowingly. We wander from the Truth. We were self-centered then, and we are still self-centered now. We choose to feast with the unwise, and subsequently make decisions in our lives that have grave consequences. I am one of those who, in the past, have aligned with the world, feasted at the table of the unwise, and chosen to wander away from the felicitous and appropriate position I have with Christ. I wandered so far away that I ended up in prison. It was the most grievous time of my life, when my choices and disobedience caused me everything that I deemed important in my life at that time. I grieved every moment and felt the most profound remorse for my selfishness, arrogance, and greed.

When you experience a moment in time when you are stripped of everything you gave value to and everything you took for granted, you have hit rock bottom. And when you are faced with what I experienced, you have very limited choices but an abundance of time. I decided to use my abundant time to draw close to God and His Word daily, because I didn't really know what else to do. I did the only thing I knew to do, given the circumstances—pray. I prayed for forgiveness, mercy, protection, especially for my loved ones, and for guidance. That was an extremely difficult time in my life, and there were days when I didn't think I'd survive. Romans 12:12 became a daily affirmation. But how do you become joyful in hope when you are confined within prison walls, surrounded by depravity and brokenness? Yes, it was an extremely difficult time in my life, and that is when I experienced the most grace from God. Yes, I committed a grievous offense, but above all, I sinned against the God I was supposed to serve. When I drew close to Him, His grace allowed me to be better and not bitter. The transformative and restorative power of God's grace opened my heart and my mind to a number of things. For one, it made me see that what I had done was not just about crime and punishment, although that was the biggest part of it in the natural, but it was also about how I had impacted lives in an adverse way, especially those I loved and cared about. I cannot undo what has been done; I can only control how I live my life going forward. I realized, too, that beating myself up and consciously subjecting myself to emotional flagellation was, in fact, pride in action. I was constantly asking for His forgiveness, yet exercising my will and punishing myself, because I could not forgive myself. We tend to forget, when we are in the middle of our circumstances, that we have a merciful and forgiving God. Our lives are not so much about what comes our way but rather about how we respond to what comes, because things will come. I was reminded of Pastor Rick Warren's TED Talk when he said, and I am paraphrasing, "Look at the hands God has given you, what are you going to do with them?" God's grace made me aware that He has indeed given me so much. With my hands, I was once again hopeful that I had something to offer that would give Him the glory. Being joyful in hope in the midst of my worst circumstance is one of the greatest demonstrations of God's transformative work in my life. It was not an easy journey, but I have never felt more hope about the promises of God than in those difficult times.

He has taught me to be patient in my affliction, and has sent people my way to encourage me to keep the faith and remind me that no matter what happens I should pray and be thankful. He constantly reminds me that He is in control of my situation and He always hears me. I may not understand why He allows certain things to happen, but He can get glory from everything in my life, in good times and in bad. The strength I have in Jesus enables me to do all things. God can turn any circumstance around and restore what was lost.

Without diminishing the fact that I broke the law and so must be punished according to the rule of law, I also believe God allowed my time in prison because He wanted time alone with me, and it was a part of His plans for my life. I am astounded by the number of prodigious people I have met during that time. I have been blessed more than I can ever articulate by the opportunity to hear their words of encouragement, experience their acts of kindness in the most deprived place I have ever known, hear their stories, and pray for them and with them. Most importantly, the women whom I have met have blessed my life beyond measure. Prison, in my opinion, is where the transformative power of love is the most evident. You see God's love in action. That is where I met the amazing people who prayed with me and for me, and subsequently allowed me to join their ministry in the community. My chapter in this book and my participation in the Embrace Women's Services prayer line are part of the restoration of God in my life. Never had I imagined that I would share my intimate moments and pain so freely and openly with anyone, especially strangers. My hope in Him encourages me to do this, because He said, *"Encourage one another,"* and if my story can encourage just one person to hold on to the hope that is in Him, then I am fulfilling part of what I am supposed to do. For Christ compels me. In 1 Peter 5:10, Apostle Paul said, *"And after you have suffered a little while, the God of all grace, who has called you to his eternal glory in Christ, will himself restore, confirm, strengthen, and establish you."*

I got to know Him deeply and intimately, every day. He taught me to be faithful in prayer. During that part of my life, my family encountered problems and catastrophic events, and I couldn't assist them. I was powerless. There were sicknesses and even the death of one of the most important persons in my life. There were also challenges within the prison walls. There were conflicts, threats, and resentments surrounding me. How do you remain faithful in prayer when everything happening around you is contrary to what you are praying and hoping for?

Life with Christ is not easy. It is a narrow road where the end is so much more than you could ever hope or pray for. But when you are in the middle of your pain and catastrophic events, it is difficult to see your end game. I remember one day when I was so distraught and broken that I got down on my knees and prayed to God and finally gave Him all my pain, sorrows, brokenness, and worries. I also thanked Him for all that He is and all that He was doing in my life, regardless of how it seemed at that moment in time. He brought me to Ephesians 6:12, which says, *"For our struggle is not against flesh and blood, but against the rulers, against the authorities, against the powers of this dark world and against the spiritual forces of evil in the heavenly realms.*" Again, I realized that being aligned with God was not easy, mostly because I had this preconceived notion of what life should be like and how things should go.

I have a predisposition to romanticize my experiences. I pray with certain expectations when I should be praying expecting that whatever the outcome is, it is according to His will. And if it is His will, then it is good. My breakthrough was the realization that I really am not in control, God is. That means giving Him all that He has given me, and telling Him that no matter what He gives or takes, I am His and that is all that matters. When I made Him my priority and started to spend time with Him, not because I needed Him to take care of my family and answer my prayers, but because I was yearning to know Him more, everything opened up. No, the prison gates did not miraculously open for me, but my eyes and my heart were able to process and see all that He was doing in my life, and it was good. The floodgates of my heart opened up, and I felt an inexplicable joy, which allowed me to see everyday miracles around me. I was in jail, and all was well. I realized how unfortunate it was that my revelation came during the most terrible time of my life, but He got my attention. I experienced being joyful in hope, and it was divine.

Our relationship with God needs daily refreshing. Spend time in His Word every day. Our role as children of God calls for discipline and sacrifice. The Holy Spirit works in all of us, and being aligned with God might mean letting some things or some people go, even when it's difficult. It may mean holding on to what we hear in prayer or in His Word that speaks directly to our hearts and translating it into action. It may mean answering the call to move beyond our comfort zones, whether it is in ministry or in leadership or in writing a chapter about our fall from grace for everyone to read. For me, I had to let go of worrying about my children, because it was consuming me and it was against what God had promised me. I needed to trust Him completely. I had to do things to please Him, not because I had to, but because I wanted to. My desire and motivation was to be close to Him and in love with Him, and Jesus became my greatest need.

Sometimes we tend to overcomplicate our lives by focusing on big things and on people, but God wants to use each and every one of us, in our everyday lives, to shine a light of hope for people when their situation feels hopeless. It could be as simple as sharing a kind word that may have significant impact on a person's life—and we may never know. We are all here as a spark of God's light, and He wants us to shine. Whatever you may be going through in your life, please remember that much like furniture being restored, the stripping is part of the process of restoration. Something or someone needed to be sanded down or sanded away. The finishing will not be as spectacular without the sanding. Always remember that we have a hope that is eternal and will never fail, and that God shines a light during the darkest times of our lives. He himself is restoring you, confirming you, strengthening you, and establishing you. Yes, we have an immutable God; He does not change. He loved us before we were formed in our mother's womb, and He knows us by name. Do not let who you are and what you have done dictate your relationship with Him. You are fearfully and wonderfully made.

My transformation is ongoing, and to be direct, this book may open my family and me to potential backlash. I prayed long and hard about sharing some of my story, and I was moved to do so. I believe my God is in full control of whatever else happens. Jesus compels me to do the right thing. My hope is to never lose my way again, so I spend time with God and His Word every day, and I surround myself with other believers, especially my sisters in Christ at Embrace. I live my life filled with gratitude for all that I am and for everything in between.

SEAT

Cry of My heart

Mirtha A. Coronel

"**A**re you there, Jesus, and do you even care?" This was the cry of my heart in 2007.

At the time, I was managing the marketing and promotional advertising for a billion-dollar business. I was married to a good man, had a beautiful three-year-old daughter, and lived in a cozy home. I was eating at fancy restaurants and exploring the world on both personal and business travels. Life was pretty amazing. To the people around me, it seemed as if I had "made it." The odds were against me, given my family's socio-economic status, the neighbourhood I grew up in, and my educational background. I was born at Etobicoke General Hospital on May 27, 1977. My parents are both of Ecuadorian descent and separately immigrated to Canada in the early 1970s. They officially met and began their relationship in Toronto. Early in my parents' marriage, they began to explore Christianity by attending one of Toronto's pioneer churches in the Spanish speaking community. I have few and very vague memories about church life as a child, because my parents stopped attending church regularly when I was about seven years old. We would only visit on special holidays, such as Christmas and Easter. I have a faint recollection of prayer being incorporated into our daily lives. However, our lifestyle did not include the daily reading of the Bible. I have a grandmother who prays, though. Her faith and prayers have been instrumental in the lives of those whom she loves, family and strangers alike. I did not know what that meant growing up, but I am so thankful for her and for every praying person who has ever lifted up a single prayer on behalf of a lost soul, a child, a youth, a marriage, a political leader, a city, a province, or a nation. There are pictures of me as a baby on the day I was presented to the Lord. I didn't know it then, but I know now, without a doubt, that the prayers of blessing prayed and declared over me on that day have been, and are still being, fulfilled for as long as I am living on Earth. Every prayer counts.

Though the neighbourhood where I grew up may not have been the greatest, our home was a good one. I was loved by my mother and father; I never doubted that. Throughout my life, there were many different people who came to stay in our four-bedroom apartment for a season and for different reasons. This environment that allowed family, friends, and some distance relatives into our home proved to be unsafe at times. At a young age, I was sexually assaulted in the privacy of my bedroom. This assault almost instantly changed my perspective of myself, changed my trust in people, particularly men, and set a stage for living in the confines of the guilt and shame that usually take root when this type of violence against sexual purity occurs.

When the offence happened, I was too scared to tell an adult. I told my best friend instead, who, in her innocence, said, "That is not true, Mirtha. Why would you say that?" In that very moment I thought to myself, *Well, if she who is my best friend, who loves me, and whom I love does not believe me, then nobody will ever believe me.* So from that day forward, I decided I would never mention it again, to anyone. That day, I believed a lie about myself. That day, in the darkness of my mind and the brokenness of my heart, the enemy of my soul planted a seed of deception. That day, I covered myself from head to toe in the filthy blanket of the enemy's lies, and my broken heart stayed hidden there for over two decades. This led to several years of living a self-destructive lifestyle.

The darkness of the thoughts within my mind and within the chambers of my heart was hidden from the unseeing eye. The person the world saw on the outside was fun and full of mirth, but on the inside I was committing spiritual, emotional, and physical suicide. I recall hiding in the darkness of my bedroom closet as a child and teenager, and hearing whispers of death spoken to me in the silence. As a young child and teenager, I had several thoughts of taking my own life, some more extreme than others. I also experimented with forms of self harm.

In 2007, I attended several special church services, and each time I went, without trying and without being able to stop myself, I would stand during the worship and tears would pour from my eyes. In addition, I would feel a powerful heat all over my being, and though I did not know what it was at the time, I knew it was something supernatural. I knew it had to do with God. It happened time and time again. During these special services, there would be an open invitation to publicly ask God for forgiveness and invite Him into your heart. Each time these invitations were made, my heart would ache, because I wanted to say yes, I wanted to take a step forward, I wanted to draw nearer to God, but every time I tried, it was as though I was wearing cement blocks as shoes. Due to the sin in my life and my unrepentant heart, the forces of darkness assigned to me had the authority to prevent me from moving in any direction. As I wept tears of grief, something began to transition in my life. I had no idea what it was or what was about to happen, but something was shifting.

One Saturday, on a warm and sunny day, my husband went to play golf with his friends, my sister took my three-year-old out, and I found myself home alone. Anyone would have seen this as a perfect opportunity for some me time or to hang out with a friend or two. However, for me, this was not the case. Through my wedding planning process, I became a form of "bridezilla" and lost most of my friends. Within two years of being married, I managed to become estranged from my two remaining girlfriends. I didn't realize it then, but God used the silence of having no close friends to make a way for Him to be my Comforter and Friend. Everyone's journey is unique. That was my path. I started to survey my home, looking for something to do; however, my house was completely in order. I had no one to tend to, and I really had nothing to do. So I began to reflect on my life. I remember thinking, *Wow, I have come a long way, but why do I feel as though something is missing?* There was a void, a great gap in my soul, a space in me that needed something that I had not tasted or seen before. I did not know what it was exactly, but I knew it was something I did not have, something that I longed for.

That day, I went into my daughter's bedroom, and I knelt at her bedside and prayed this simple prayer: "Dear Jesus, if you are out there, and if you really care, release me from the shackles of this world. I want to know you more. If you hear me, please send me a sign." Within ten minutes of saying that prayer, I heard a knock on the door and it was a Witness of Jehovah. I immediately knew in my heart that I was not going to become a Jehovah's Witness, but I also knew that this was the sign I had asked for in prayer (Psalm 51:17 MSG). I looked up and chuckled, saying to God, "You have a sense of humour." I opened the door and invited them in. They chatted with me for a little while and left a yellow book for me to read. I read the yellow book on my way to work, and after a few days, I told my husband about the visitors and the book. He turned to me and said, "If you want to know about God, why don't you read the Bible?"

Some time later, my brother and sister, who attended a church together, invited me to another "special service;" this one was being led by the youth of their church. I remember being at the service and observing the youth and the way they passionately poured out their hearts to Jesus as they spoke and sang. I thought to myself, *When I was their age in high school, I knew what I was doing on a Saturday evening and it didn't look or sound or feel like this.* I thought, *If these youth who are in the toughest years of life, transitioning from childhood to young adulthood, while going to high school, are here worshipping Jesus, what's my excuse? I am a grown woman—I am married, I have a daughter—yet I need what they have. This time, when they offer that special invitation to come to the front to make a public confession and to ask for forgiveness of my sins, I am going to go up. This time, there will be nothing to hold me back.* So I waited and waited, ready to jump on the opportunity to say yes to Jesus, but the call never came. Instead, as the service wrapped up, they asked all the youth to come forward so that a prayer of blessing could be prayed over them. Immediately, I began to make my way to the front, as I had determined in my heart that I was not leaving that place without my blessing. As I stood at the altar, one of the youth leaders saw me, and I know that the Holy Spirit in him revealed that I was there for more than a prayer of blessing. He knew that I was ready to repent and ask God for forgiveness of my sins and to invite Him into my heart to be my Lord and Saviour. It was amazing to learn, years later, that he had been praying with my brother and sister, along with others, for our family and for the salvation of my soul. Furthermore, it was fascinating to me to learn that the youth leader that ran the service had been praying and fasting for three months, asking God to allow at least one soul to be saved during that service. Incredibly, more stunning to me is that I discovered in 2017 that the special service was held on September 22, 2007, which on the Jewish calendar was Yom Kippur, the Day of Atonement.

Since that day, I have not looked back but have pressed forward, fighting the good fight of faith and running the race. I intentionally set my heart to know the Lord, reading His Word and praying to Him. A few years later, I was praying and telling God that I wanted to know Him more. I was asking Him to remove all the things that hinder love. At around the same time, I received another invitation to attend a church service being held in the basement apartment of a home. They had a special guest that day, a powerful woman of God. After her sermon, she began to minister to God's people through prayer. I was standing at the back of the small room, partially hidden behind a cupboard, when suddenly I heard her speak these words, "I lift off of you the dirty blanket of your childhood." I know she was just speaking what the Lord was revealing to her. What she did not know was that she was directly speaking to me, and I could see and feel the dirty blanket of guilt and shame that had plagued me for over twenty years being lifted off of me. That week, I felt the freedom to confess my sins to the Lord in a way I had never felt before that time. I began to share with Him the guilt and pain that I had been feeling. I repented of the specific sins that came to my heart and mind, and I began to forgive each person that was involved in any sinful experience in my life and all those who had hurt me along the way. This process took the better part of a week. By the end of the week, I felt free, but then I realized I had one more person to forgive, and that person was me. I had to forgive myself. New air was breathed into me that day, and strength and courage and faith arose in me in increased measure. For the first time in my life, I had the freedom to share my testimony with a trusted friend. My God is so good.

Someone said to me recently, "Your life fascinates me. What happened? How come this God thing works on some people and not on others?" I shared part of my story, and the person said, "I've tried many times, been there, done that. I have woken up after a night of irresponsible behaviour and said, 'This is it. This is the last time. I will never do this thing or that thing ever again,' and yet a week later I am in the same place doing the same thing."

I do not know what fears are hidden in man's heart; I only know that when I set out on this journey, I did not set out to change my ways or to change myself, I set out on a journey to get to know God. I had lived my life knowing about God just like I know about the many celebrities whose careers and lifestyles I followed, but just like I do not personally know any celebrities, I personally did not know God. My transformation journey required one indispensable key, and that is His Word, for it is the River of Living Water. It has the power to cut through bone and marrow, soul and spirit. Without His Word, I might have turned around and changed some of my ways and become a better person; however, it would have been in my own strength and in my own ability. It would have been without faith. Faith comes from hearing the message, and the message is heard through the Word of God.

Our minds need to be transformed into the likeness of Christ. Our success is not based on our accomplishments; our success is based on being good stewards of all He has given to us and living a purposeful and purpose-filled life. His Word enables us to learn the language we need in order to pray effective prayers that are like the pen of a ready writer ready, to write out and live out our destiny as we mature and grow and walk in it. His Word is a healing balm to our soul, healing the deep wounds of our heart. In His Word, because He is His Word, we are able to find a friend and comforter. His presence is our home and better is one day in His presence than one thousand elsewhere.

This was the cry of my heart in 2007: "Are you there, Jesus, and do you even care?"

The LORD heard the cry of my heart, and He has shown me that not only is He real but that He also loves me. *"GOD told them, 'I've never quit loving you and never will. Expect love, love, and more love! And so now I'll start over with you and build you up again...'"* (Jeremiah 31:3–4 MSG).

SEAT

My Gift from God

Siobhan Bent

"The test came back positive."

Silence.

"Are you still there, Siobhan?"

I can still remember my exact location when the secretary told me that I was pregnant. She confirmed what the dollar-store pregnancy test had already told me the day before, but I didn't want to believe it was true. In that moment, my mind began to race, my heart quickened its pace, and the tears began to run down my face. I was going to be a mother.

My seat at this table occupies the space of truth

and transparency with my experience thus far in motherhood. My experience has been filled with a wide range of feelings, such as doubt, fear, and a bit of anger at times, but also joy, excitement, and an abundance of love. You see, when I was younger, I decided that motherhood was something that would not be a part of my life's journey. I didn't have any real reason other than it was my choice, and I chose not to. But during my pregnancy, the Lord began to reveal some things to me that I did not recognize as the root cause of this decision.

I am the first child for both my mother and my father, and I was born when they were just fifteen and sixteen years old, respectively, still children themselves. Most sixteen-year-olds were doing what the typical teenager was expected to do—going to school, getting their first job, or learning how to drive—but not them. Life as they knew it, or even hoped it to be, was drastically shifted into another direction that neither of them was prepared for. Their relationship as a couple did not last very long, and to be honest, to this day I do not know what happened between them. What I do know is that Mother made the decision to leave the relationship and raise me on her own, which she did exceptionally well. My father, on the other hand, made his decision to be non-existent in my childhood. As a result, I have no childhood memories of me and my parents together. As I grew older and more aware of his absence in my life, I became hurt and angry, because I could not understand why a parent would do such a thing. Is a child not a gift and a reward from God? I began to resent him. Then I suppressed the hurt and built a barrier around my mind and my heart. I just could not understand it, so rather than living with the hurt and confusion, I developed an I-do-not-care attitude towards him and everything concerning him. I did not need or even want him to be a part of my life. He was pretty much dead to me.

My mother was all I had. She was my everything. If I were to describe my mom, I would simply say she is the best. She did the best she could with what she knew while raising me, considering she was just a child herself. I wish I could give a better description of my mom, but that's all there is to it. She was the best teacher, the best cook, the best provider, and the best inspiration to me. Her strength and resilience inspired me the most. No matter what life threw at her, she always pushed through to ensure that we—I also had a younger brother and sister—were well taken care of. We had a stable home, were never short of food, were always well-dressed, took yearly family vacations, knew our Lord and Saviour, and went to church every Sunday. Everything was taken of, and she did it by herself.

As the eldest, my mom was very strict with me, because I was a "girl child." That did not make any sense to me, so I felt like being a girl was a curse, and I was paying the price by having to cook, clean, and help take care of my younger siblings. That sounds absurd, right? I can laugh at this now, but back then it was not funny at all, and most times it was the cause of the most challenging moments in our relationship. These were times when the woman whom I loved and admired so much was the last person I wanted to see or be in the same house with. It was in those challenging moments that I would lock myself in my room or leave the house and go next door to my neighbour's, just to get away from her and the hurtful things she would say to me. When my mom was angry or frustrated, one of the things she would say was, "If I had just listened to Joyce, I would ah dash you weh." Translation: she would have had an abortion. Who is Joyce, you ask? Joyce is my grandmother, may her soul rest in peace. She was my mom's mother, who had her own parenting issues, but that story is for another book. Hearing these words from my mom's mouth, on top of my father's absence and neglect, made me feel like a mistake. Do you remember that I had made the decision to never be a mother? Well, this feeling is why I made that choice. I was engrossed in the fear of having those same feelings I thought my parents had about me.

I loved children, all children. I loved them so much I managed to get eleven godchildren of my own, most of whom are grown adults now but will forever be my little babies. Children are innocent and are subject to whatever lifestyle their parents provide for them. I did not want that responsibility neither did I want to risk making a child feel the way my parents made me feel.

As I began to mature and evolve into my own self, I realized the time had come for me to spread my wings, separate myself from Mom, and begin to tackle this thing called life as an adult. In the initial stages of my transition, there was a strain in my relationship with my mom, but over time we both realized it was necessary. My mom needed to see the years of her hard work and sacrifices—I prefer to call them investments—manifest into the ambitious and courageous young woman that I had become. But I also needed to see for myself that all those years of curfews and tight restrictions were truly intended to mold me and not just stifle me. That was a very happy time in my life; I owned my own home, I was working, I was paying my own bills, and I was living life on my own terms. Life was good, or at least I thought it was.

I was never a very social or outgoing person. I was always the quiet one in the room, seen but not heard. I had a small circle of friends and usually could be found at home or work, minus the few years I spent in basement parties and dancehall clubs. I spent a lot of time by myself, most of the time I was completely okay with that, and then other times I felt like I didn't have anyone I could reach out to when I wanted to talk. I found myself in emotionless relationships with men that I knew cared for me but whom I could not see a long-term future with. I allowed them to be in my life to fill the loneliness gap I had. I no longer recognized myself. Even though everything on the outside seemed normal, I was fading inside.

April of 2012 was when I got the confirmation that I was going to be a mother. An avalanche of emotions began flowing through my body, and I instantly started to shiver as if I were standing outside in the dead of winter in minus-twenty-degree weather. I wasn't, though, because it was a warm spring day, and I was in my car exiting off Highway 401 eastbound and heading onto highway 400 northbound, right where the road has the rippled pavement to help slow you down as you make the curve. I was in shock. I was scared. I was embarrassed. Most of all, I was disappointed in myself. How could I let this happen to me? I was not married. I was not in a financial position to care for a baby. I was not married. Yes, I know, I said that already. But that was what was going through my head while the tears fell down my face. *Why is this happening? I am not capable enough to be someone's mother. How am I going to do this?* These questions and feelings of doubt were non-stop throughout my entire pregnancy. Despite the abundance of love and support I received from my friends, family, sisters in Christ, and my pastor, I was still very disappointed in myself.

Then one day, the Holy Spirit reminded me that in 1 Thessalonians 5:18 it says, *"Give thanks in every circumstance, for this is God's will for you in Christ Jesus."* And that is what I had to do, every day. I gave God thanks, because He doesn't make mistakes. I was pregnant with purpose, and this was going to be my time to heal all the hurt and pain I had bottled up inside of me. He protected both me and my baby, and I had an amazingly healthy pregnancy and gave birth on December 28, 2012 to a healthy prince, Matteo, which means "Gift of God."

For a long time, I had a different vision for my life than what God was handing me, and to be honest, because I want to be transparent, it wasn't an easy transition. However, instead of being disappointed and depressed, I decided that I had to meet God where He was, because motherhood was the calling and purpose He had for my life. I needed to learn how to embrace this stage of life with confidence, boldness, joy, passion, and, most importantly, purpose and intention. It took some time for me to get to this place of acceptance, but I know that in all things God works for the good of those who love Him, who have been called according to His purpose (Romans 8:28 NIV). Now that I'm here, my focus is being the best mom I can be to my son in the ministry of motherhood. If I care for myself spiritually, mentally, physically, and financially, I can be there for my son, be there happily, be there with joy, and teach him to do the same. I know that God wants me to be successful as a mom and business owner but not just for me; He wants me to uplift and empower other moms across the world to find the same joy in the ministry of motherhood.

"Children are a heritage from the LORD, offspring a reward from him. Like arrows in the hands of a warrior are children born in one's youth" (Psalm 127:3-4 NIV).

A letter to my son:

Dear Matteo,

When God gave you to me, He knew
that I needed you.
I needed you to learn how to love,
again.
I needed you to show me what joy was,
again.
I needed you to feel happiness, again.
I needed you to be whole, again.
Son, you are indeed my greatest
achievement, and I promise to love you
forever.
Thank you for making me a better me.
Thank you for being my gift from God.

Your mom,

Siobhan Bent

SEAT

Mentally In~~sane~~ Faith

Naomi C. McBean

"Mommy! Daddy!" I shouted when the lights went out, but unfortunately for me my cries were too faint. No one heard me as I stood in the dark, trapped between the clothing racks within the department store. It seemed like five minutes, maybe ten. All I knew was that a three-year-old little girl was alone and afraid, and neither of my parents nor any of the staff from the department store could find me. It must have been about three hours later before I was rescued from what I now call "the first entry point."

You are probably wondering what I am talking about. It was at that very moment, at the age of three, while trapped between the clothing racks, that the spirit of fear entered my spirit, occupied my mind, and manifested itself in the form of claustrophobia— an abnormal fear of being in small spaces. I do not remember my parents ever addressing this new-found fear or even discerning it, but I do remember frequently getting trapped in my childhood apartment elevators, and my parents and siblings not understanding why I would always opt to take the stairs or not sit in the backseat of our vehicles. I'll admit they were a little frustrated, but let us excuse their ignorance, because not even I, between the ages of three and fourteen, could explain my quickened heart rate, my shortness of breath, or the dreadful feeling that filled my mental space every time I saw an elevator, suitcase, or closet. Yes, even a suitcase or closet. I am sure my babysitter locking me in the closet at the age of eleven and my siblings always playing in suitcases fed this dreadful fear of small spaces. By the age of fourteen, I was not locking the doors to my private washroom at home or even public washroom stalls. The fear just kept growing.

I remember by the age of fifteen I began recognizing this feeling that would come over me as soon as September and the cooler months approached. It was the feeling of loneliness. This feeling would always lead me to believe that I was very much alone, even in the company of family and friends. I could not figure it out, because this feeling only showed up once September hit. One day, sometime in October, while over at my cousin's house, I remember saying, "There is that feeling again," but this time the feeling was slightly more intense, a bit heavier. I remember it was late in the evening, and my cousin, her friends, and I decided to take a stroll to the nearby park, and while they were sharing in laughter and being silly like teenage girls should, I was feeling trapped within the earth. I vividly remember gazing into the night sky and feeling boxed in. Of course, I did not mention my feelings or thoughts to anyone there. Instead, I continued to smile, while fear filled my body, occupied my mind, and manifested itself in the form of seasonal affective depression—a type of depression that is related to the change in seasons.

Still undiagnosed, I continued to experience life as a teenager by creating small safety nets, which included not taking elevators, not locking doors, and ensuring that I kept myself busy during the fall and winter seasons. I was no different from any other teenager who believed that they had it all under control. My plan was working. I had everything under control, until about age sixteen. This was the age when some of my friends and I decided to try marijuana. Despite the positivity my culture has promoted surrounding the use of marijuana, my experience with it was not so positive at all. In fact, it was quite damaging.

One day after school, my friends and I rolled up our "spliff," otherwise known as a "joint." It was all fun and games until the high hit me. I was no longer laughing; I was actually screaming while my friends were still laughing at me. I was trapped. I felt trapped within myself. I could not breathe. My heart was racing, and the feeling of death was nearby. I remember screaming at my friends to get me out, but how could they get me out of myself? So they continued to laugh, while fear filled my body, occupied my mind, and manifested itself in the form of an anxiety attack—an emotional, psychological, or physical response to high degrees of stress and fear. Unfortunately for me, my mental health took a turn for the worse at that point.

It was about three months later that I was sitting in my living room watching TV, when suddenly shortness of breath, heart palpitations, and the intense feeling of danger consumed my body. I quickly ran into my bathroom and just gazed at myself in the mirror. I knew it was my way of affirming my reality and dispelling the surreal feeling I was experiencing. I was having another anxiety attack. I am still not sure what triggered it that evening. A short while after, maybe some days, weeks, or even months later, I was lying in my bed, worrying and over-thinking about my traumatic experience with marijuana, and before I knew it, I felt this sharp snap in my brain. I did not think anything of it at the time, but the next day things did not feel the same.

The next afternoon, my friends visited and again engaged in smoking marijuana, and even though I did not participate, my heart started palpitating. I was experiencing shortness of breath and fear, and the shouts followed. I was screaming at my friends, telling them they had done something to me. Mind you, we were not in an enclosed area, neither was I directly with them while they smoked, but the smell of marijuana triggered fear, occupied my mind, and manifested itself in the form of PTSD—a mental health condition that is triggered by a traumatic event. I honestly felt in my mind that I was tripping, simply from smelling the marijuana. That fear persisted for many years. Every time I encountered the smell of marijuana, it brought me back to my very first encounter with it. My brain would perceive danger, and I would run away from the situation in terror. This obviously affected my social life. I began withdrawing from family and friends. I was not only avoiding elevators and locked doors, but I was also trying to avoid the smell of marijuana, which was very hard to do in my environment. Even the smell of a skunk would send me into an anxiety attack and trigger the PTSD.

I later found a remedy to deal with my social life and anxiety. I began drinking excessively in order to cope. I remember thinking that as long as I had alcohol, I would be mentally shielded from the fear, anxiety, and PTSD. As you guessed, the alcohol was only a temporary fix. My excessive drinking eventually developed into paranoia. My mental health was declining at a rapid rate. I was fearful of eating, shaking people's hands, visiting friends and family, attending social gatherings, and the list goes on. I thought everything had drugs in it. I went from a size ten to a size zero very quickly. I was uneasy, depressed, and on the verge of cracking. I expected to be admitted in a mental health institution or die. My friends and family did not understand the alarming decline in my mental health, because I still showered, smiled, and did everything that a functional individual apparently does.

This fear had taken root at a young age and had manifested itself in various forms: claustrophobia, anxiety, panic attacks, paranoia, PTSD, all kinds of mental conditions, disorders, and illnesses, and all of my coping methods were exhausted. My saviour alcohol was working against me, and my doctor too. He told me, "I am sorry. There is nothing else I can do for you." I remember leaving my doctor's office feeling betrayed and defeated. After all, no medication, psychiatrist, psychologist, psychotherapist, or self-help group seemed to be working. They all seemed to be working against me; at least that was how I felt. I had tried everything, but yet, mentally, I could not get it together. I was desperate. I walked away from my career, my relationships, and my doctor. I was being tormented mentally and needed a way out. I needed an answer. I needed more than a prayer.

In 2014, I met a lady, and she finally introduced me to an amazing psychotherapist, someone who was able to help me begin the cognitive-behavioural therapy that I needed to help break free from the bondage of fear. This individual was a healer. She introduced me to a man named Jesus Christ, and I decided to accept the invitation to sit at His table. Of course, I thought I would be made whole instantaneously. I was whole, but I did not understand the power of belief, nor Jesus' power, authority, and all that was given to me upon my rebirth. I was a disciple of Christ, struggling with my mental health. "Is that even possible?" you ask. Yes, it is.

I remember driving home one evening, and the smell of the skunk's spray triggered an anxiety attack.

I began driving erratically. I could not figure out why I was still experiencing these attacks; after all, my thoughts were now subjected to the lordship of Jesus Christ. But God reminded me that my body was filled up, and like a sick person, throwing up eradicates the body of the filth. In my case, it was fear. He reminded me that there was a process that He was taking me through, so I began to interrogate fear. I read every scripture in the Bible about fear, and I quickly learned that *"God has not given us the spirit of fear; but of power, and of love, and of a sound mind"* (2 Timothy 1:7). I had a sound mind, which was my declaration as I began to meditate upon His words. The attacks came, and each time they came, I recited that very same scripture. Soon, I noticed that the length of my attacks began to decrease. They went from an hour to thirty minutes to fifteen minutes; the process of renewing my mind was transpiring. I was actively using the Word of God, which is alive and active, to combat my fears.

There were different occurrences that took place, where I could see God acting as the strong tower in my mind. I vividly saw and felt God not allowing my natural thoughts to escape me or go further than the standard He had raised. I was applying His words by *"Casting down imaginations, and every high thing that exalteth itself against the knowledge of God, and bringing into captivity every thought to the obedience of Christ"* (2 Corinthians 10:5).

This four-year journey has been hills and valleys, but as I continue to *"be anxious for nothing,"* I encourage you to do the same (Philippians 4:6-7). I was never intentional about stopping the use of alcohol as my shield, but four years later I am alcohol free. I do not know how and when it happened, but God. So do not be afraid to let go of all of your safety nets and toxic coping strategies, *"for God is our shield and our exceedingly great reward"* (Genesis 15:1). Everything else is only a coping strategy; Jesus Christ is the cure! Allow Him to take your broken thoughts through His "neuro-sanctification process" (Dr. Helen Noh). To remain "mentally in-faith" we must do as the writer Paul instructs: *"Be transformed by the renewing of your mind"* (Romans 12:2).

"Finally, brethren, whatever things are true, whatever things are noble, whatever things are just, whatever things are pure, whatever things are lovely, whatever things are of good report, if there is any virtue and if there is anything praiseworthy—meditate on these things" (Philippians 4:8).

Love, Naomi,
Mentally In-Faith

SEAT

The Prodigal Daughter

Atisha Sanderson

There I was in that same situation, again; a capital "L" had been imprinted on my life yet another time. I couldn't help but think, *God must not like me. Is God seeing this? Will God save me from this? God, just make it stop! Make them stop, please. How could this happen to me all over again? Another loss!* At that point in my life, grief and loss seemed to always be my portion. I lost my husband at the age of twenty-seven to a very aggressive type of cancer of the thoracic spine. At the time of his death, I had an eight-year-old, a four-year-old, and a nine-month-old baby, all girls. Ten years later,

I was pregnant again and facing almost the same heart-wrenching reality of loss. This time, I was grieving someone who was alive. This pregnancy was supposed to be a joyous experience, but instead it turned into a nightmare.

I am not sure if I was grieving the loss of the relationship or the fact that I was facing the open embarrassment of having a relationship end during a time when I needed all the comfort I could use. I began to compare my deceased husband with my son's father, even though there was no real comparison. I also tortured myself by rehearsing the last time I bore a child and how terrible it was to have a young baby and a dying husband. I hosted pity parties very often. I felt robbed. Life isn't a movie; there is no rewind button, neither is there a fast-forward button, and I definitely wasn't the one holding the remote control. If I were, I would have tried using those particular commands. Abandonment was my greatest fear, and now I was facing single motherhood, but in hindsight I realize that I was actually never alone.

When you are in a relationship with someone, whether it is romantic or platonic, the goal is to be like-minded. You pour into them, and they pour back into you. You speak, they listen; they speak, you listen. It's an agreement and a commitment to build each other up. Imagine developing a relationship with someone who only comes to you when they need something, or they only pay attention to you when they are in need of your time or your ear. When things are going well with them you don't hear from them, but when they are in need of you they come crying, asking for help. How would you feel? Not good, I assume. If someone treated you like that it would probably make you feel mistreated. Well, I thank God that He is not like man, because I am guilty as charged. That is how I treated God—like that good old friend that will always be there for me, no matter what. My relationship with God was conditional on my part and not on His. I have four children, as I mentioned earlier. If any of them were to get hurt, I couldn't bear to witness it. Can you imagine how God feels when we, as His children, fall down in the walk of life? Especially if we fall as a result of disobedience. Having to sit silently and allow your child to make that mistake, knowing that they have to learn on their own, must hurt. When we hurt, God hurts.

After I had my son, Prince, I had mixed emotions. I was very happy to have had my first son, but I was also very anxious and depressed. I experienced deep-rooted feelings of abandonment and rejection. I was battling against the spirit of hopelessness. I self-loathed a lot, allowing alcohol and cigarettes to become a magical problem solver. Like using a magic wand, I probably uttered "Abracadabra" in my intoxicated state, but nothing magical materialized. So I just kept consuming the alcohol, hoping for relief. I was in disbelief. There was a picture painted with promises; then there was the harsh reality that was contrary to my preconceived notions.

One day I went to the doctor and asked for a referral to a psychotherapist. I was fearful that I was losing my mind. I had stopped breastfeeding, but I didn't tell the doctor why, because I was too ashamed. At the time, alcohol seemed like the best coping method. I was drinking almost a bottle of red wine a day. The following day, however, the pain, mental anguish, and self-loathing would always return. My problems were never solved, they were only magnified.

During this time, I could not pray. Everyone around me would say, "Atisha, pray." I could not pick up the Bible. I stopped communicating with God. I was in a hole of depression and despair so deep that I thought if things didn't get under control soon it would be like heading downhill at high speed with no brakes.

I remember one day calling the Embrace prayer line, which is designed for women who need spiritual uplifting and a warm embrace. I knew I needed God, but there were so many strongholds. Strongholds are things in your life that the enemy uses to keep you in bondage. In my case, addiction was a generational stronghold in my life, because my father was a former drug addict. I remember holding a cup of wine in my hand as I listened in on the call. The speaker began to encourage the group, referring to 1 Peter 5:8. This scripture is about being sober-minded and vigilant, because the devil is like a roaring lion seeking whom to devour. Instantly, I felt my shoulder drop, because I was silently ashamed. Those words reached into the depths of my spirit. I knew God was speaking directly to me, but a battle was simultaneously occurring in the realm of the spirit. This battle was a spiritual ploy to distract and cause interference with my communion with God. I had to empty myself and allow God to fill me with His Spirit, again. I was desperate for change. It was in my desperation that God's plan for my vertical alignment began to manifest.

Unexpectedly, God strategically caused some key

relationships in my life to simultaneously sever. He shifted some things so I would be forced to depend on Him alone. What a friend I have in Jesus. I tried to resist, but He was clear. After a while, I stopped challenging Him. Obviously, He knew better. He would do a better job running my life than I could. When God has a plan for your life, it's only so long and far that you can run before He pulls the carpet from under your feet. I have had the carpet pulled from under my feet several times in my life. A situation will repeat itself until the lesson is thoroughly learned. I may have had my own ambitions and plans, but they only included God when I met a problem on the road of life. What I failed to acknowledge was that God designed my life's roadmap, and He had the correct direction and blueprint. I think God probably laughs at me when I act as if I know it all, when He already sees everything that's ahead and knows so much more than I do.

When He starts exposing things, it's very hard to deny His presence. He does not let up. Thankfully, He is relentless in His pursuit. The information that I was made privy to through divine connections led me to the understanding that the relationship with my son's father was irreparable. I could neither sweep this under the rug nor place a Band-Aid on the sore. My sisters in Christ would encourage me to talk to God and "cry out to Him." So one day I did. Remarkably, He stepped in and rescued me. I remember the evening I attended a conference called The Prophetic Shift. I remember feeling determined to attend, because the headline spoke to me, and I needed a good shaking and shifting. That night, I encountered the life-altering power of God, through a very prominent woman of God. The Lord would have her tell me these words: "You are too good of a person to be walking around feeling this way. I heard your cry, and I'm going to fix it. I will deal with everybody who has caused you pain." At that time, all I needed to know was that I was in the thoughts of God and that He loved me and was going to save me. I wasn't feeling quite loveable. Instantly, I bellowed from deep within my soul. In that moment, a tidal wave of past hurts and everything I had been through resurfaced. It was as though all of my pain and suffering was being opposed by something, or someone, much stronger than I, driving the anguish out of me. Self-pity, agony, my personal dress rehearsals of hurt, and the replaying of the scenarios of blame and contentions were leaving me, supernaturally.

When God touched me, it seemed like everything stopped hurting. I immediately stopped drinking. The smoking stopped. There was no more desire to do these things. I noticed joy re-entering my life, filling the empty rooms where pain and shame had been evicted. There was a new calm in my life. Doors began to close where the enemy used to gain entrance into my life, like my rollercoaster of emotions, other people's opinions, and my addictions. When I say other people's opinions, I mean in all areas. It may sound simple, but when you have a relationship with the Holy Spirit you become reliant on His direction rather than the opinions of five different individuals with five different personalities, standards, and beliefs.

When I began to immerse myself in prayer and to take the time to bask in His presence, my life took on a sudden shift. I started to see myself as God sees me— as who I am and who I was created to be. God taught me how to walk in total forgiveness. I was in God's surgical theatre of healing and deliverance. I spoke to the enemy that had kept me bound, and echoed the word "Flee!" When God gets our permission to work, He does a perfect thing. He has no abandoned jobs. I learned to stand confident, strong, and restored in Christ. My very environment changed. The once hostile atmosphere of war turned into peaceful plains. Favour over my life was restored. I spoke about many doors being closed by God, but they are nothing compared to the doors that God has opened for me. Time belongs to God. I am accelerating spiritually from one level to the next. It's like I was catapulted from one season to another in order to make up for the time that I lost when I veered off the course. I was given restitution. I now walk in the authority that God has given to me.

I have experienced healing and deliverance, witnessed miracles, experienced the grace of God, accumulated uncountable testimonies, and there are still many more to come. At times I cry out to God, no longer from a place of despair but from gratitude. I am thankful to God for picking me up, healing me, emptying me, cleansing me, and filling me. I am honoured to be a vessel used by God. As my life has been shifted, my stance has also shifted. I am standing firmly in a place of purpose and victory. There is nothing like the knowledge and love of God.

Due to my experiences, I now have a greater understanding of Deuteronomy 28, which outlines the blessings for obedience and the curses for disobedience. I have come to the realization that my walk with Christ requires a total surrender to His will and purpose. Not my will, not my desire, not my ambitions, but His navigation. Christianity isn't a walk in the park; there are trials and tribulations, but it has its rewards. The greatest reward is Salvation, a covenant between God and humanity that I would not trade for the world.

SEAT

From Poverty to Riches

Bernice Moreau

I was born of black Roman Catholic parents, Felix and Sybil Moreau, on the Caribbean island of Trinidad, as part of a historically imported society comprised of African, East Indian, Chinese, and European peoples. It can be said that "mixture is the texture of the island." In order to understand the significant events that made me who I am today, it is necessary for me to introduce the socio-religious and socio-economic setting into which I was born. My young parents and older brother were relatively poor but very religious. We lived in a home owned by another person.

The journey of my life is divided into four distinct mileposts: early childhood, teenage years; young adulthood, and aging adulthood. The one word that triggers my memory of my past is the word *poverty*. In my life story, the concept of poverty is not merely a deprivation of money and material things, but is more of a deprivation of social, emotional, psychological, and mental stability during the early developmental stages of my life. The spirit of poverty entered my life in my mother's womb when my maternal grandmother passed away suddenly, fifteen days before I was born. Her passing affected my mother and her family so badly that I was immediately seen, not as a beautiful baby girl, but as one who brought great sorrow to this young family.

To make matters worse, as if to prove my family and the entire Roman Catholic community correct, my father, the only person who welcomed my presence in this world, my caregiver and comforter, took ill. He was an engineer on the train. One day after work, he was riding home and got soaked in the rain. He immediately contracted pneumonia, an incurable disease at that time. He died eleven days later with me, his six-month-old baby girl, in his arms. It was immediately decided that I was a bad omen, that my life brought sickness, death, and financial poverty for the family. The spirit of poverty robbed me of my mother's love. It was commonly said that I killed both her mother and her husband. To put it mildly, everyone believed that my mother, older brother, and I were doomed for life because of my birth. I was rejected, left to myself, deprived of hugs, kisses, and cuddles, which babies need to develop a positive outlook on life. My early childhood experiences were detailed to me years later by my mother and others on her side of the family. I was unknown to my father's family, since my paternal grandparents died when my dad was young, and he grew up with relatives in a distant community unknown to my mother. The spirit of poverty overshadowed the foundational stage of my early life. When I was three, my young, physically beautiful mother married again. Her new husband was of East Indian descent. They lived in a predominantly East Indian community, away from my mother's relatives. My older brother was adopted by one of my mother's sisters, as was the custom then, and my mother kept me with her new family.

My mother's marriage began with great difficulties, because she was black, Roman Catholic, poor, had a black child from her first marriage, and unaccepted by his family because their union was against the customs and traditions of the East Indian community. I remember the shock I felt when I became consciously aware of my place in a family where my mother and I were different and unwanted. The situation became worse with the addition of four other children by my East Indian stepfather and black mother.

I was born in a community that was superstitious and very conscious of the presence, power, and possession of evil spirits. The purpose of religion there was to protect true Roman Catholics from being destroyed by evil spirits. There were two dominant religious groups in the community I grew up in: the Hindus and the Roman Catholics, with several other Protestant religious groups trying to win souls from the major groups. My teenage experiences that I was keenly aware of consisted of the physical and emotional differences between my younger siblings and myself. I experienced blatant racism, sexism, poverty of every type, and rejection and subjection by many of my teachers and leading adults in the community. I was whipped for acts I did not commit. My true friends were few. The spirit of poverty dominated every area of my life.

The experiences I considered joyful and happy were few and far between. One of the better times I had was when my mother would put me on the train and send me off to spend holidays with one of my favourite aunts and her family. There I met my older brother and cousins who looked like me. After seven years of marriage, my stepfather suddenly became a serious and violent alcoholic. Our family went through a time of hardship and violence that I cannot easily describe. It was literally hell on Earth in our home, and my stepfather's siblings and family rejoiced and said, "Now this nigger family will break up." They wanted all that my stepfather had then. My late-teenage, early-adult years were extremely difficult, to the point where I dreaded living. Death was more appealing. Fear, rejection, deprivation, and physical abuse were my constant companions, and I hated myself. I had a very poor self-esteem and self-worth. Earlier in my life, other people saw me as black, tall, skinny, ugly, quiet, shy, scared, and the list goes on. As a teenager, that is how I viewed myself also, so death was most welcome if it would take life from me.

In spite of my mother's financially poor social existence and her distressfully unhappy home, she sent us to school, to her church, and taught us to pray the Roman Catholic way. With all that was going on in my unpleasant life, believe it or not, school was the only bright spot in my life. I had two teachers—a female, Teacher Ver, and a male, Teacher George. They were my life support. They took a liking for me, and Teacher Ver taught me what it was to be a teenager becoming a young woman, while Teacher George not only helped me with my school work but also encouraged and assisted me in knowing myself. He protected me from those male teachers who were ready to take advantage of my naivety. I began to love the classrooms where I was accepted, encouraged, and taught. It was in the classrooms of my two favourite teachers that the spirit of poverty was challenged. Slowly, I began to realize that there were those who were willing to love me in spite of my deep-rooted poverty and all the negative ways the community perceived me. I began to change the way I looked at myself and who I could become.

Another very beautiful thing that happened was one of our neighbours recognized that we were not Bible-believing Christians, and she began to ask my mother to send us to a small Brethren church not far away from our home. Believe it or not, this Christian, born-again woman pleaded with my mother for one year to send us to Sunday school, and my mother refused because of the strict religious laws of the Roman Catholic Church. I believe the neighbour was praying for us, because one Sunday after service at the Roman Catholic church, I ran away and attended the Brethren Sunday school. It was the first time in my life that I really understood the gospel message, and what caught my attention was the love that Jesus had for me. If He could love a "nobody" like me so much that he died for me, then I could live for Him. I was so convinced that what I was being taught was truth that I was convicted by the Holy Spirit, and right there and then I committed my life to Jesus Christ. Like the woman at the well in John 4, I went home and told my mother. I was whipped for my disobedience. However, the whipping could not hold me back. I ran away every Sunday afternoon, and whenever I was caught I told my mother that I would leave home and she would not see me again, even if I had to live on the street. She saw how fearless I was and realized that my behaviour was not my natural, fearful, nervous way of behaving and submitting. God spoke to her heart, and she allowed me to attend the Sunday school. I was given my first Bible, and I read it from beginning to end in a few months. After that, I read the Bible once a year from cover to cover. I began to learn how to pray and to read the Bible to my brothers and sisters. Of the six of us, four are now saved, and my mother and stepfather passed away saved.

After successfully completing junior high school, I took the entrance exam for high school and won a scholarship with books. However, I could not attend high school, because my mother could not afford to pay for three different sets of uniforms, the cost of travelling, my lunches, and the school educational trips. I began searching for work, and I was allowed to teach the kindergarten kids at a private school. The money that I earned I used to pay for six high school correspondence courses from London University Preparatory School in England. In my young adulthood, I was blessed with a son, whom I took care of with the help of God, my church brethren, and my family. During that period of my life, my great God gave me the opportunity to acquire, free of charge, several levels of formal post-secondary education. I received a scholarship to Teacher's College in St. Lucia, under the auspices of the University of the West Indies. I also received a Commonwealth scholarship to the University of Liverpool, where I studied teaching at the first school level; a Bachelor of Arts with Honours; a Master's in Sociology at Dalhousie University; a Master's in Christian World View at Christian University; and a PhD from University of Toronto in Sociology of Education. While I was in the process of completing my PhD at the University of Toronto, I was privileged to receive a one-year fellowship at the University of New Brunswick to gather the data for my thesis, which I completed with honours. I taught at Dalhousie University in Nova Scotia, Carleton University in Ottawa, Ontario, and Tyndale University College in Toronto, Ontario. I have now retired from formal academic teaching and am regarded as an adjunct professor with Carleton University.

My earliest knowledge of God began with the Roman Catholics, but I met God personally through the Brethren in Trinidad. I followed the way with the Black Baptists in Toronto and eventually with the Church of God in Ottawa and in Mississauga, Ontario. I was under the leadership of Apostle Canute B. Blake, who was then the pastor of the Ottawa Church of God where I met Sister Claudia Clarke, the church secretary. She invited me to the services at Ottawa Church of God, and Bishop Blake prophesied that I would become a clergy minister. I laughed at his prediction, but God had a plan similar to his. Under Bishop Blake's leadership, I studied the required Christian education programs, the church's history, and the doctrinal beliefs of the Church of God. I successfully completed the requirements for ordination and the necessary license to be a clergy minister under the auspices of the Church of God International in the USA. Here I am, twenty seven years later, in ministry at New Life Covenant Centre (NLCC), under the leadership of Apostle Canute B. Blake.

As I come to the end of my journey, I can say with confidence that God has healed me of the deep-rooted negative spirit of poverty that plagued my life for many years. I am free, and I am still in the classroom teaching the Word of God to others. The Lord has given me His promise that when I am poor, in Him I am rich (2 Corinthians 6:10). And even when I experience some of the types of poverty that may attack me, I can, and I do believe that I make others rich in faith through Jesus Christ, my Lord (James 2:5).

SEAT

When Disability Challenges Faith

Susan Stewart

It's quite amazing how things have changed from thirteen years ago. I suffered a brain injury sustained in an accident, and it left me with challenges in my balance and my vision. The effects of my injury require the use of various aids in order for me to function on a day-to-day basis. My accommodations consist of voice recording for typing, visual aids, such as large fonts, in order for me to read, and consciously moving at a slower pace to meet the deficiency in my mobility. I haven't driven since the accident, as I don't feel entirely physically able. Therefore, I utilize public transportation in order to get around. Those are the light effects of my injury, but I want to talk about some of the heavier stuff affecting my life today.

Living with the stigma of a brain injury, regardless of how it was acquired, is a mentally debilitating shadow I battle with on a daily basis. At times, I want to shout to the world, "I am the same person! My brain just moves slower. I want to be treated as the same person that I was. I want to be heard. What I have to say matters as much as the people who do not have disabilities." But this is not the case.

Prior to my accident, I was a sought-after athlete, highly regarded as a Canadian basketball Olympian. I was respected and looked up to. Then in April 2005, my life as I knew it was literally smashed, and the life of disability began. In my book *Unbreakable*, I describe the journey through rehabilitation. I went from living the life of a world-class basketball athlete to the life of a frail brain-injured patient confined to a bed in a hospital room, having to learn how to walk, talk, and simply live again.

The journey through rehab was challenging, with so much to learn, but I was up for the challenge. The athlete in me knew all about hard work and dedication to achieve goals set before me. My season of rehab reminded me of an athletic training camp. The purpose of athletic training is to prepare us for the actual competition. I was surrounded by caring therapists, family members, and friendly cheerleaders, and everyone worked simultaneously to get me home and functioning independently, again. But what I didn't know then was the enormity of what I would face after rehab ended. After going home and settling into my new norm, the harsh reality of living with disability started, and for me this new reality has been the match of my life.

The world outside of my family, community, and therapists has been a fierce battle. Now strangers everywhere are being introduced to my physical shortcomings and limitations, and too often my getting acquainted with unfamiliar people has been less than welcoming. I have been labelled, mistreated, and often overlooked. In a society bursting with information, it amazes me how unaware we are about the needs of those living with a disability.

The Honourable Kirsty Duncan, Minister of Science and Minister of Sport and Persons with Disabilities for the Government of Canada, stated that "People with disabilities must advocate for themselves and are tasked with the responsibilities to educate the public and bring awareness to their plight." I completely agree. The ministry's mandate strongly speaks of inclusion for all, including people with disabilities, and yet this is far from my lived experience so far. People truly need to be educated and made aware of the challenges people with disabilities face on a daily basis and understand the emotional toll we experience from feeling inadequate in a society that makes us believe that we are.

Travelling by public transportation alone exposes

the sad reality that we live in a time when chivalry has definitely departed. It is very seldom that anyone offers me their seat in the bus, and sometimes, it is disheartening. I took a flight recently. Due to the long wait time, I approached the counter to inquire whether there was a delay and how long the wait might be. Because my speech is somewhat slow, the airline representative asked me if I had been drinking, to which I answered "No," and carried on with my question. I may not have said anything about being disabled, but she made me painfully aware that I am. I felt terrible and insulted. These days, these types of human responses no longer illicit a reaction, because I feel emotionally numb. Having said that, of course it hurts me, but I find explaining *"No, I am not drunk, I have a disability"* on a regular basis is worse than showing my emotional responses.

Navigating the world of disability also involves finding and keeping gainful employment. This, too, has been a troubling exercise of the will for me. When I actually found a job, it wasn't long before I was let go due to "downsizing." Well, that was the excuse they gave me. On the surface, stigma is not obvious; however, the judgements associated with disability have denied me, and countless others like me, job opportunities. Like me, many talented candidates are left feeling invisible and unwelcome in the workforce. The barriers to employment are real.

To combat some of these barriers I figured that going back to school could help close potential education gaps. A higher education would be key to not only landing a good job but also keeping one. If I could be retrained, certainly I could access new opportunities. Why exclude myself from available opportunities such as school? I sought out this avenue and here's what I found: presently, there is no funding for people with disabilities to go back to school that I qualify for. I consider myself a fairly resourceful, hardworking, and determined person, yet I can't seem to shake the feeling of being perpetually left behind. I realize that how I respond to the day-to-day behaviour of society is not the norm; however, the way I must handle it is by faith. My faith must play a bigger role, in that, the Bible tells us to pray about everything. I pray about the ignorance I consistently face, and I place it in God's hands. Going to church, continuing the fellowship with the brethren, and keeping my focus on Christ keeps me focused on the love I am getting from my God and how He is seeing me through. What He says about me is way more important than what the world is saying about me. Therefore, I've come to realize that I really am not behind; I am simply on a relentless pursuit of my destiny. The path God has chosen for me requires the help and participation of my family, friends, service providers, church members, community, and society at large.

When we open our spirit, we are able to see the needs of our brothers and sisters. We have eyes and ears to sense when our neighbour is hurting. I remember receiving a call from a church sister. She called to invite me out to the movies. She felt the need to do it for me. I thought it was so nice of her- we did and I enjoyed her company and being engaged socially. After that experience I realized the pleasure it brought me and I am grateful. I hope that more people would give their time for people like this.

Devoting time and effort to disabled persons go a long way. If we could do more of that as a church community, we would be a better church. Galatians 6:2 instructs us to *"Carry each other's burdens, and in this way you will fulfill the law of Christ"* (NIV). By paying more attention to the idea that disabled persons are people who seek to be included and recognized respectfully, we can break the cycle of discrimination, poverty, and hopelessness that seeks to invade our lives. The parable of the great banquet found in Luke 14:12-14 challenges us to reconsider those we may have forgotten. *"He said also to the man who had invited him, 'When you give a dinner or a banquet, do not invite your friends or your brothers or your relatives or rich neighbors, lest they also invite you in return and you be repaid. But when you give a feast, invite the poor, the crippled, the lame, the blind, and you will be blessed, because they cannot repay you. For you will be repaid at the resurrection of the just'"* (ESV). While I value the help and love of others, I look to the Lord as my ultimate source. I am supported by family and friends, and I am very thankful for that. Sometimes they, too, may not understand the sensitivities and emotions I feel, but God brings me back to focus on their genuine love for me.

This is my truth. Living with a disability has a range of societal impairments that accompany it. Whether it is the feeling of invisibility, the lack of sensitivity, or society's shortcoming in offering a seat to someone less mobile, I am learning to cope a little better every day. I seek God to find new ways of doing what I used to do, and I am discovering things I have never experienced before. The Lord promises, *"My grace is sufficient for you, for my power is made perfect in weakness"* (2 Corinthians 12:9 NIV). Therefore, I will boast all the more gladly about my weaknesses, so that Christ's power may rest on me.

Today I boldly use my voice to advocate for those who are not able to speak for themselves. I have dared to share my story with anyone who will listen. If you are living with a disability and you are wondering how to cope from day to day, I leave you with this scripture that has helped me, *"May the God of all grace, who called us to His eternal glory by Christ Jesus, after you have suffered a while, perfect, establish, strengthen, and settle you"* (1 Peter 5:10 NIV).

SEAT

Journey to Him

Lorena Williams

The moment we enter into the world, our spirit man yearns for Him, and as we grow from little girls to women, we search for Him, until He satisfies our thirst.

Will you find Him?

The journey I embarked on to get to Him was one that many never make it through. "Looking for love in all the wrong places" may sound like a cliché, but there is much truth in that statement. When the attributes of love are presented to you in a twisted and distorted manner, the journey to true love will take you to all the wrong places. Once you discover what the purpose of love is, you can start a healthy journey of healing, reconciliation, and finding a satisfying relationship. I can confidently tell you that the only way to experience a fulfilling life and a fulfilling relationship is by allowing God to use you to display His glory and by allowing Him to be your sufficient source.

I found my way to Him after twenty-five years, and I discovered that I had a Father who loved me unconditionally, and a Groom that was madly in love with me. I found God and His son, Jesus. I can confidently say I am a child of God, the wife of an amazing man, the mother of three beautiful children, and a proud business owner of The Gospel Café and GC Jerk Xpress.

In the beginning of my journey to Him, the only description I had of myself was that of a lost child. Growing up without the example of a father or a man that had a relationship with God, and growing up watching my mother struggle as a single mother to four girls caused me to make my own twisted conclusion about what a father and a husband should be. And at the age of eighteen, I allowed a man to dictate and mold my concept of what a relationship should look like. That man is now my husband, but only by the grace of God. Collin is a son of God, an amazing husband, and a wonderful father of five amazing children. We now have a marriage that honours God and displays the love of God. Many take marriage in the church lightly, not realizing that marriage is a great gift and responsibility. We now understand that marriage is meant to be a display of God's *agape* love. Marriage is to display patience, forgiveness, joy, peace, unconditional love, and all the wonderful attributes of God to the world. It's a gift that you are meant to enjoy and take great care of, until death do you part.

Many say marriage is work. I personally don't like to use that word, because I now see it as a gift from God. Think about it: how can a gift from God be work? That would not be a gift, it would be a curse. This is the seed that the enemy plants in the minds of married couples after the honeymoon stage of a relationship. Pastor Bobby Sommers said, "How can you value and appreciate anything given to you if you don't understand the purpose?" This statement changed my entire perspective on life and all that it has to offer. If you don't read the instructions to a new computer, a cell phone, or a laundry machine, how can you ever truly experience and enjoy the fullness of what that thing has to offer? Now, think of your spouse, your children, your parents, your co-workers, your pastor, we have not been trained to understand the purpose of those relationships, so we never truly understand the value they have.

The Word of God has become my constitution, my guide to a way of living that honours God. However, that was not always my reality. My journey to marrying the love of my life was only fulfilled after I made the decision to find the only Him that really matters. The day I made Jesus my Lord, my eyes were opened and I made a U-turn. This was the journey that led me to Him.

Our situation growing up, from the womb to

adulthood, can sometimes subconsciously cause us to make some crazy choices in life. I believe my journey to God started the day I met Collin. We both worked at McDonald's in two different locations. My head manager was being transferred, and Collin was taking over. We can never forget the day we met. I was visiting the manager that was leaving my location at his new store and, as we were talking, Collin walked right into our conversation. The manager that was being replaced by Collin said, "Don't worry, Lorena, you will like Collin." And Collin replied, "No, you won't just like me, you are going to love me one day." I was definitely not happy about that response, but he was speaking it into existence without even knowing it.

When we began our relationship, I was so happy that I was with a man that was an amazing father to his girls, a mature man that had a good job, a man that I thought was treating me well. Our relationship soon became painful, because I wanted more, and Collin didn't know what more was. He had been in two failed relationships with the mothers of his daughters, and now he was in a relationship with someone twelve years younger than he was. What could he offer, and what could I want more of, when we didn't have God in our hearts and we didn't have the example of a wife or husband growing up? What could we offer each other when we didn't understand the purpose of our roles?

I was living with a man who literally dictated and molded my way of thinking. I made Collin my God, and my purpose then was to keep him happy. I did whatever I had to do to keep him from leaving our relationship. When a relationship becomes this toxic, you begin to lose yourself—you no longer know who you are, you have no voice, and you start to live with no life. After so many years of being in an unhealthy relationship and having my first daughter at the age of twenty, I began to not only live for Collin but also for a beautiful baby girl that needed all of me. The relationship became more stressful, because my attention was no longer on him. I was living like a single mom, but living with my daughter's father. We began to live two separate lives, and my sadness was great. I started going out with my coworkers, who insisted I was young and should be having fun. I was never the kind to go clubbing or drinking or have fun, unless I was out with Collin. But after months of going out with friends, there was no fulfillment. I began to talk to the God people spoke about; I somehow knew He was there.

Collin got invited to a church on Easter Sunday. He was up early getting ready, when I woke up and asked where he was going. "I'm taking my aunt to church," he said.

I then asked, "Can I go?"

"For what? Stay home with the baby," he said.

I insisted, and he eventually agreed. It was that day that I finally found Him. Jesus was there, I felt Him. I remember trying to keep my composure, but I wanted to explode with joy. He was presented to me perfectly, and I wanted more of Him. I remember feeling like this about Collin at the beginning of our relationship, but that did not last, because he was not perfect, but Jesus is. I left that service with tears rolling down my eyes. "What's wrong with you? Why are you crying?"

Collin asked in an angry tone.

"I don't know," I responded.

He began to laugh.

I continued in my pursuit of getting to know this Jesus for myself. The Word began to quench my thirst for the truth. I completely fell in love with Him. I felt a love I'd never known. Collin began to get jealous, because I was going to church on a weekly basis, and I was not showing the same interest in him. He began to make comments like, "This church thing is a joke thing," and "you will soon get bored of it," amongst other things to discourage me from going to church.

The Word began to open my eyes to see my life from an entirely new perspective. The desire to please God was birthed in me, and I felt uncomfortable living and being intimate with Collin. I felt as though Collin was not deserving of me anymore. I made a decision that I would get out of the living situation I was in with Collin, but I struggled with becoming a single mother and having my daughter grow up without her father, the way I did. The only thing I could think of was letting Collin know that I was not comfortable living with him anymore, because it was not pleasing to God. This was my well-prepared speech to him: "Collin, first I want you to know that I love you and I want to continue a relationship with you. I want our daughter to grow up with you by her side; however, now that I have Jesus in my life, I'm no longer comfortable living with you without being married. This is not an ultimatum, but I just want you to know that if you have no intention of marrying me that's okay. I just need to know so I can move on with my life. I'm not saying I will leave tomorrow, but if you can't make a decision anytime soon, one day you will come home and we will not be here." Collin didn't say anything; he just listened and walked away.

I thank God that even though Collin was submerged in the things of this world, after a few months, on New Year's Eve, he proposed. I was happy but still very concerned that I was going to marry a man who had not accepted Jesus as his Lord and Saviour. In Corinthians 6:14, the Word warns us, *"Be you not unequally yoked together with unbelievers: for what fellowship has righteousness with unrighteousness? And what partnership has light with darkness?"* I know this scripture didn't directly apply to my situation, because we met when we were both in the world, but after several years of being with him I surrendered my life to God. Collin wanted nothing to do with God. His exact words were, "When I decide I want a boring life, I will become a Christian." I prayed and pleaded with the Spirit of God that if I was making the wrong choice by marrying Collin, then He should give me a clear sign. I was willing to walk away from Collin for God. I got to a place where God was everything to me, and I trusted Him completely. I was like a small child unwilling to make a decision without my daddy's consent. After much contemplation, I felt great peace with my decision to marry Collin. I was completely trusting God to do His part in Collin's salvation.

I now know that the enemy was trying everything in his power to discourage my walk with God. After a few months of being engaged to Collin, I found out I was expecting another child. I was happy but felt convicted, because I was extremely sick during the beginning of the pregnancy. I began to think God was punishing me for staying in the same living situation with Collin after we got engaged. I left the church I was a part of and ignored my pastor's wife's phone calls. She was so persistent that she left several messages and even visited my work place to find me. I finally picked up the phone one day when I was feeling extremely ill from morning sickness, and her sweet voice said, "Sweetheart, what's going on? Where have you been? I miss you." I then told her I was pregnant, and she was so happy for me. I mention this because I am so grateful that I had such a supportive church family during this difficult time.

Collin and I got married on January 28, 2006. I was water baptized on January 29, 2006, and we had our son on March 4, 2006. I was now married with two kids and saved by the grace of God, so the only thing missing was the salvation of my husband. I did not realize the new journey I was embarking on; in my mind, this was God's part, and it was going to be easy. Living with an unsaved husband was hell on Earth. I now understand the scripture about being unequally yoked. We were living in two different worlds. It is impossible to be with someone who doesn't have a relationship with God. It's like living in a war zone, never agreeing on anything—finances, children, music, work, family, you name it, we could never agree. I now had a voice, because I had Jesus, so I became rebellious. I began to pray with the wrong heart. My prayers were "Lord, make Collin stop gambling. Make Collin stop going out so much. Make Collin stop being so mean to me." The prayers I was praying were selfish; they were all about me. Instead of drawing Collin closer to God and allowing God to use me, I became angry and distant, even though I was declaring and believing for his salvation. I had to repent and renew my thinking towards Collin's salvation.

The salvation of a loved one is not about us, it's about God's glory. I began on the journey of my life, because my life depended on it. I was unwilling to accept defeat. I completely committed myself as a vessel for God to use in any way to help in the salvation of my husband. I clung to the Word of God and began declaring, *"As for me and my household, we shall serve the Lord"* (Joshua 24:15). *"Likewise, wives, be subject to your own husbands, so that even if some do not obey the word, they may be won without a word by the conduct of their wives"* (1 Peter 3:1). *"Ask the Lord of the harvest, therefore, to send out laborers into his harvest"* (Matthew 9:38). *"And this is the confidence that we have towards him, that if we ask anything according to his will he hears us"* (1 John 5:14).

Our trials became greater once we got married. I understood that the enemy despised marriage because it is a reflection of God's love, and he is threatened by it. So I continued to press in, even when it felt like what I was doing was in vain. As Collin slept, I would lay my hand on his heart and on his head, and I would say, "Lord, I thank you that Collin has already surrendered his life to you. I declare that his mind, heart, and spirit will be sold out to you, and that his will will always be your will." I would pray this over him every night, and I would wake up expecting the manifestation of all I was believing for. My faith was definitely tested, but I began to get so radical that my own family would say that I was believing for the impossible. That just fueled me more. I was out to prove my faithful and my amazing God. I began to participate in early morning corporate payer every morning at five o'clock. I would drive to Scarborough from Etobicoke, completely fueled. I believe that trials are an opportunity to strengthen our relationship with God. I became completely dependent on God. There was no man on Earth that was going to help me get through this difficult time.

One morning, after eight months of attending five o'clock morning prayer, I got up at four o'clock as I was accustomed to doing every day. As I was about to leave, I clearly heard the Spirit say, "Go and get your husband." I questioned what I was hearing, because for eight months I wanted Collin to attend corporate prayer with me. I remember responding to the voice and saying, "But, Lord, he just came home two hours ago." Collin was a gambler. He would often gamble until the early hours of the morning. I was sure that he would refuse, but I did it anyway, out of obedience to God. I went into the room and whispered close to his ear, "Collin, I know you just came home and you are probably tired, but I was hoping that you would come with me to corporate prayer. I really feel you should come with me today."

There was a moment of silence, and then he responded, "What's wrong with you? I'm not going. I'm tired."

I left the room, disappointed. As I was about to lock

the door, the Spirit of God spoke again and said, "Go back and get your husband." I stood at the door and struggled with the idea of going back into the room, but out of obedience I was willing to do it. As I was approaching the room, I saw the bedroom light on. I slowly opened the room door and saw Collin in the bathroom brushing his teeth. I asked, "Did you change your mind?" And he replied, "Just give me a minute."

As we drove to the meeting, there was complete silence. I did not want to say anything that would make him change his mind. We arrived, and as the meeting was ending, the visiting pastor from China pointed at Collin and said, "You over there, you stubborn spirit, stay after the meeting. I would like to have a word with you." As you can imagine, I was so afraid of how Collin would react. But to my surprise, he agreed to stay behind after the meeting. The pastor asked if he could visit our home, and Collin agreed. To this day, I have never asked Collin what he and the pastor spoke about. I was expecting the manifestation of his salvation, so I was excited that something was happening.

Collin began attending church with me after that meeting, and about two weeks later, Collin surrendered his life to the Lord. It was the beginning of my new life with my believing husband. All the prayers manifested. God used His labourers to plant seeds in Collin, and everyone in my household continued to serve the Lord.

Believing for the salvation of your spouse is the will of God. Any desire you have that aligns to the will of God must manifest. Become radical about your desire; speak it, believe it, and trust with all your heart that what you are expecting must manifest.

As a wife, it is vital that your husband bears witness to the God in you. Set your eyes on God and pray and thank God for your husband daily. Declare that his eyes are always set on God and that his relationship with God is intensifying daily. It may seem like work, but be mindful that the enemy is like a roaring lion seeking whom he may devour, and as wives it is our responsibility to cover our husbands, as it is our husbands' responsibility to cover us. Pray daily for his strength and be willing to submit to the God in him.

After Collin surrendered his life to God, we embarked on a new journey together, which forced us to start a marriage the way God wanted. And one piece at a time, God was able to build a strong foundation in our marriage, a foundation that would not be broken. I want to be transparent by saying it was not easy. When we were both serving God, the enemy tried everything to see our marriage fail, but who God puts together, no man or devil can pull apart.

When speaking to other wives, I always start by reminding them that God is no respecter of persons. What He did for me, He will do for you. There is a spiritual formula, and as you follow it, the result will be the same.

SEAT

Jackie E. Nugent

las, you made it to the 13th seat. What I omitted from the information in the beginning of this book is that the 13th seat is empty. No one occupies this space, yet. This chair remains vacant, because it has been reserved for someone very special, and that special someone is you. Yes, you!

You are invited to take your seat at the table, and in the words of my friend Dr. Andrew Blackwood, we are delighted to have saved a space for you. It is here that you can also begin to revive your personal testimony and table talk journey by participating in the 13th seat challenge. By inserting your story here, you dare to become a part of an unending narrative of hope to the people within your sphere of influence.

It is here that you become a part of the eternal movement of believers all over the world who dare to testify. Whether you are a stay-at-home mother, a full-time government worker, or a young person simply searching for meaning, your story matters. What you bring to the table is significant.

If you are uncertain or wondering how or where to start, here's a helpful table talk starter activity that embodies the basic concept of this book. You can try it as a part of your personal journal entry or perhaps you may want to gather with a group or a few friends around the "table" like we did. Remember that the table can be a real table or simply a symbolic place.

When the co-authors and I began this journey, I asked them to answer this table talk question: "What chair represents your story?" The responses were phenomenal. Their heartfelt answers became the foundation on which each woman wrote her chapter.

Allow me to reintroduce each coauthor. This time, take note of the chair she has chosen and how each chair or seat coincides with each woman's journey.

Siobhan Bent:
The Transparent Chair

My journey to motherhood has been filled with a mixture of good, great, and, sad to say, bad emotions. Feelings I am aware I've had but have neglected to embrace for fear of being judged or criticized. My chair represents transparency. Why? Because it's time for me to share my truth about how the relationship with my mother has impacted me, my role as mother to my son, and my role as an encourager of other mothers in the community. I refuse to remain silent and confined to the opinions of my critics, real or perceived, including the critic within me. Transparency unlocks truth, and the truth will set you free.

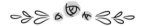

Amber Shurr-Sloss:
The Church Pew

The church pew is classic. Throughout the generations, there is a comfort and a feeling of coming home associated with the church pew. It is strong and solid. It is meant to be a place that accommodates many, rather than an individual identity. There is a strong expectation that the church pew will deliver what is right and expected. The church pew is nailed down, expected to stay in its spot and do what it is supposed to do. It is used for limited purposes and can sometimes be deemed outdated and old-fashioned. The church pew has the expectation of always having the Word (Bible) and a song (hymnal) and not showing the wear and tear of use and abuse. The church pew has a commanding presence for the benefit of its occupants.

These are the attributes of the church pew that my story relates to.

So to my fellow pews, sitting in church, strong, silent, showing no wear or abuse, to whom others turn to for strength and support, while you are silently broken and battered on the inside, know that God sees you, God hears your cries, and God knows the aching in your soul. You are never alone. You matter and your story matters, because it is God's story. Find a way to tell His story through you.

The World Did Not Deserve Her

The world did not deserve her, all it wanted was her strength
Demanding all her smiles, giving timelines to her pain
The world did not deserve her, her view naïve and free
The life she tended carefully and lived so vulnerably
The world did not deserve her, all it wanted were her songs
Her silence was too deafening, for she did not belong
The world did not deserve her, all it wanted was her skin
It threw away the heartbeat that pounded deep within
The world did not deserve her, it told her to be tough
But left her crushed and broken when her strength was not enough
The world did not deserve her, for her passion was too much

Her laughter and her tears, the way that she could love
The world did not deserve her, condensing highs and
lows
Only celebrating when she went with their flow
The world did not deserve her, but it wanted her to use
Her worth was calculated in the things that she could
do
The world did not deserve her, she so needed to know
That the world did not deserve her, 'cuz this world was
not her home.

~ Amber

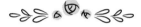

Yolando Robinson:
The Park Bench

Why the park bench? That is a good question. It was the first thing my mind saw when asked what seat I would choose for my story. You see, that seat represents a stillness that comes when I am there. It represents a peace that I believe is God's gift to me during challenging moments. The park bench is the seat that seemingly beckons me to come and sit with God. It is almost like an invitation specially made for me. Me, Him, and that wooded park bench surrounded by the beauty of the trees that could say so much about all they have seen. It is here that God calls me to rest in His sweetness and reminds me of the beauty of all His creation, including me.

Elle Leaño:
The Comfy Recliner

In my home, the recliner is my family's comfy place. My children and I have spent countless hours in it, enjoying movies, sports events, and priceless talks about some things and also about nothing. Looking in from the outside, it may seem somewhat ordinary, even mundane, yet it's my favourite chair. It represents a huge part of my life, the memorable moments with my children, who are the most beautiful expression of God's love in my life.

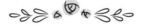

Susan Stewart:
The Metal Folding Chair

The chair that best represents this season of my life is the metal folding chair. When folded up, it isn't sturdy, and it seems useless, like my injury. But once it is unfolded and locked into place, it is strong enough to hold even the heaviest person, just like the issues and stressors of life. Can fire burn through metal? No kerosene fire can burn hot enough to melt steel. Unfold the iron in me! Iron unfolded stands. Extend the iron in me, Lord.

Narkie Assimeh:
The Fiery Chair, a.k.a the Hot Seat

When I think about a chair and what it usually represents, comfort, relaxation, and taking a break come to mind. Choosing the "chair on fire" or the "hot seat" illustrates how uncomfortable my situation has been. It seems that in the last few years, in my personal and work life, I have always been in the hot seat, feeling that expectations have been laid on me and me alone. When I was planning my mom's funeral in a foreign country or trying to maneuver through the invisible barriers to return to work, I couldn't just sit and relax, because if I did, I'd be burnt. If my mom's home-going wasn't planned well, I'd be burnt with embarrassment, shaming myself and my father. I'd be burnt for being in financial disarray, burnt for not doing all I could to get back to work. I was in a place I didn't consider home, planning a funeral without the typical resources, and having to fulfill cultural responsibilities that most in the western world would not understand.

The heat from the seat represents my fear of embarrassment, fear of misrepresenting or showing disrespect towards my culture and its rituals, and the fear of being swallowed by my grief and not being able to shoulder the responsibilities of effectively planning my mother's home-going. My chair symbolizes not being able to sit back and truly relax and take a moment to grieve my loss.

Naomi C. McBean:
The Psychologist's Chair

I chose the chair of a psychologist because this chair has a triple meaning for me. This chair speaks to the issues of the mind—distorted thoughts, fears, and phobias— issues I have dealt with since childhood. This chair automatically draws my attention to the previous interactions between me and my former psychologists, psychotherapists, and psychiatrists. It is such a vivid reminder of how my perspective was dominated from the patient's chair and how I viewed my everyday psychology.

This chair reminds me of how, through the Word of God, I was transformed by the renewing of my mind (Romans 12:2) by bringing every thought into captivity to the obedience of Christ (2 Corinthians 10:5). Now, with a shifted perspective, this chair is a reminder that I am still sitting in the psychologist's chair, but something has changed. My perspective has shifted from the patient to the psychiatrist's perspective. Through God's grace, which is sufficient, I am now studying the discipline of psychology to earn my Bachelor of Arts Degree.

Atisha Sanderson:
The Rollercoaster Seat

The chair I chose is a rollercoaster seat. This seat best describes the pattern of my past life, which was always like an unpredictable rollercoaster ride. My life was known for its series of escalating ups and plummeting lows with a number of sharp jolts between each transition. My wonderland is not the famous amusement park found in Toronto, Canada, rather it is a place of uncertainty, without any sense of security. It is a place where I relied on mankind to provide the things that only Christ could offer. It is a place where I often found myself lost, because there is no direction there. Wonderland is a place of hopelessness for me. But one day I chose to give up my season's pass to the thrills of wonderland and yield to the call of God on my life.

When I raised my standard of living and made the decision to walk with Christ, I also switched rides. This time I knew that my course was preordained. I knew that my steps would be in alignment with the will of God. In no way do I imply that the terrains aren't still rough on this ride called life, but now my seatbelt of obedience is securely fastened, and I have God as my co-traveller. He has proven Himself faithful in keeping me safe and sound.

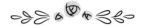

Lorena Williams:
The Picnic Bench

The design of the picnic bench is timeless and durable, and its foundation is strong, strong enough to withstand the worst of conditions and never lose the purpose of the original design. Collin and I had our first date on the picnic bench. Our relationship is similar to the design of a park bench. With God being the foundation, we have been able to endure and withstand the worst of situations and the original plan God had for our relationship still remains the same.

Jackie E. Nugent:
The Car Passenger Seat

A life lived without meaning is like driving aimlessly, going nowhere, especially if you find yourself in the passenger seat. I had a misconception of who I was, which caused me to be driven and tossed to and from anywhere the wind would blow. Unable to distinguish my true identity from the counterfeit demands of my destructive world system, I simply sat back and allowed people, places, things, and circumstances to determine my destiny. As a result, I squandered much of my life void of divine purpose. Then I accepted a better way of living—the Kingdom lifestyle. I learned that I was royalty and that what God said in Jeremiah 29:11 was also a message for me: *"For I know the plans I have for you," declares the Lord, "plans to prosper you and not to harm you, plans to give you hope and a future"* (NIV).

The promises of God gave me the significance, value, and security I was longing for. I am no longer a passenger in getaway cars, literally and figuratively, carelessly running for my life. I now allow Jesus to direct me in all I do. Even though I still remain in the passenger seat, my driver has changed. A life once driven by forces of darkness and sin is now driven by God, the sovereign driving force of my life. I can depend on this driver and can confidently say, "Where He leads me, I will follow."

Dr. Bernice Moreau:
The Classroom Chair

Between the ages of ten and twelve, the classroom was where I found joy. It was there that two teachers, one male and one female, taught me. The female teacher was a Christian who went beyond the book and taught me about my personal care, while the male teacher treated me like a little sister. They loved me and helped to fuel my love for teaching. The chair I sat in extended beyond the walls of the classroom. You see, my passion for teaching began long before I became a teacher, and resulted in my first students being the trees, bushes, and the grass in my countryside neighbourhood.

Mirtha A. Coronel:
The Early Childhood Transition Chair

I choose the early childhood transition chair to represent my chapter. Many of us, though grown adults, are like children with unique needs, and the multifunctional, multipurpose chair is easy to set up (for success), easy to adjust (as we mature), easy to use in a classroom (our mind and worldview), in a clinic (our heart), or at home (our soul in the stillness of His presence). In our place of being children with various needs, He equips us to be multifunctional, multifaceted, humble, practical, and useful instruments in His hands. When we trust God and allow ourselves to be cared for and led by His Spirit, He enables us powerfully. In order to mature in Him, we need to begin with accepting how much we need Him.

Now you have heard our testimonies and the place in which we have been seated. As an introduction to your table talk or personal testimony, I would like to pose the same question to you. Describe a chair or seat that represents your story. Explain why or how it ties to your past, present, or future story. Finally, think about how God has liberated you from or within your circumstances. This simple exercise can ignite powerful table talks and testimonies in your home, with friends, social groups, or your congregation.

Here are a few guidelines to having meaningful table talks.

Know that everyone has something to bring to the table and is welcome to do so.

At the table, we exercise good table manners. For example, we have respectful dialogue and caring interchanges.

There are no hired waiters or waitresses. We serve one another with heaping love garnished with patience and seasoned with kindness. We believe Matthew 23:11, which says, *"But he who is greatest among you shall be your servant"* (NKJV).

At the table, conversation is key. Engage in thought-provoking questions that will stimulate *conversation about your story. I encourage you to write your raw answers to the questions, because you may need to edit them for future use. This is your story, your testimony, so share it.

Finally, at the table we are equals. There is no big seat or little seat, dignitaries or otherwise. Like you, we are simply twelve women with life-altering testimonies, sharing about a God who continues to transform our lives every day.

Here are four more tips to maximize sharing your testimony:

1. Anticipate change. The place you are seated can change. In other words, what you are facing today will not last forever.
2. Always leave space at your table for someone else. God never intended for anyone to journey alone. As you may see yourself looking outside from within, someone may be looking in from the outside, seeking a place of safety and belonging. Make room to help others and for others to help you, too.
3. Testimonies are fuel that ignites greater passion and fire for God in your life and in the lives of others. Never underestimate the power of your testimony. Believers who are on fire for God often cause others to catch on fire, too. Your story may just be the fuel of hope and revival that someone who is discouraged, devoid of hope, or who finds themselves out of fellowship needs. Like an ember tossed outside of the fire, your testimony may spark a faith revival and reignite a desire for Christ.
4. You are a credible witness. You just have to open your mouth and share your story. No one knows your story like you do. Your encounter with the Lord is personal, yet your experience must not be kept to yourself. Do you remember when God came to your rescue? You knew it was He who soothed your aching soul and met your needs. What was the encounter like for

you? How did you feel during or afterward? Did you cry, like me? Or were you silenced in reverence and awe?

Our desire is that everyone reading this book will be energized by the Holy Spirit to share, and as testimonies about the saving grace of Jesus spreads across the world, revival will follow. Right where you are, the Holy Spirit is with you to empower you to witness.

"And they overcame him by the blood of the Lamb and by the word of their testimony..." (Revelation 12:11 NKJV)

God wants to use you like a passageway to lead others to His eternal love. There are too many people who have given up their place at the table to sit in the seats of shame, deception, and despair, when there is an honourable seat already reserved for them. Like the story of Seth in 1 Samuel 9, it is time to accept the invitation and sit at the King's table. What an honourable offer and privilege it is to be invited to sit with the King, not just for a day or two, but as an heir, to live within the domain of the Kingdom, forever.

King David's invitation to Seth reminds us that we, too, are invited to the Lord's table. Jesus is the King of kings and Lord of lords and is inviting us to dine with Him as heirs. This may seem farfetched for some of us, because, in light of where we have been, we do not see ourselves worthy of such an honourable position. We acknowledge the public and secret tales attached to our flaws, faults, and failures. Figuratively, parts of us are crippled, like Seth, leaving us to wonder how and why someone would choose us. Yet God, in all His majesty and love, sees beyond our faults and sees exactly what we need. Imagine Seth sitting at the king's table. As he is seated there, perhaps with other members of royalty, envision the table as it becomes a great equalizer. It is an equalizer because while Seth remains seated at the table, his disability is hidden and he looks like everyone else seated around the table.

Today, if you will confess that you are imperfect and have missed the mark, then you are confessing that you, like all of mankind, have sinned. *"For all have sinned and fallen short of the glory of God"* (Romans 3:23). We are sinful, and *"the wages of sin is death"* (Romans 6:23). Since God is Holy, and we in our natural state cannot measure up to His perfect standard, we need a Saviour, an Equalizer to hide and cover our sins. The Bible teaches us that the Lord Jesus, the only perfect One that ever lived, is ready and willing to forgive us and purify us of all of our sins and gift us with eternal life. Regardless of where we have been, crippled or dropped like Seth, in despair or perhaps left alone soliciting for help, Jesus is relentlessly pursuing you to offer restoration and an eternal seat as an heir at His table.

Your seat, however, cannot be earned by good works. It is given as a gift when you believe in the finished work that Jesus did when He died on the cross for the sins of the world. *"For God so loved the world that He gave His only begotten Son, that whoever believes in Him should not perish but have everlasting life"* (John 3:16). If you have not experienced the eternal life found in Christ, we extend the invitation to you right now.

Through the sacrifice of Jesus, the love of God has bridged the gap of separation between mankind and Himself caused by sin. All are invited to cross the bridge into the family of God and accept Christ's free gift of salvation. The Bible says, *"But as many as received Him, to them He gave the right to become children of God"* (John 1:12). If you will receive the invitation of eternal love, the Lord will come in and dine with you now and for eternity at the heavenly banqueting table where a seat is already prepared for you. If you will accept the invitation, I invite you to pray this simple prayer:

Heavenly Father, I confess that I am a sinner. I ask for Your forgiveness. I believe Jesus died for my sins, has risen from the dead, and is now alive, mediating for me. I will trust You and follow You as my Lord and Saviour. I invite You into my life now. Be my constant guide, and help and strengthen me to do Your will. Thank you. Amen.

"The Lord is near to all who call upon Him, to all who call upon Him in truth. He will fulfill the desire of those who fear Him; He also will hear their cry and save them" (Psalm 145:18-19). If you prayed with sincerity of heart, you now have access to God's eternal inheritance of love for you.

Beloved, *I AM* your Restorer, your Healer and your Redeemer. I want to heal the marred image and identity that the world has impressed upon you. If you are willing, I am ready. I will realign that which is out of order and resolve the unfinished in your life. For in My presence there is freedom, joy, and peace. In My presence, there is a wellspring overflowing with

126

unconditional love, waiting for you to partake.

You are empowered by God to testify with authenticity about your encounter, even if you are a new believer. In John 4, a Samaritan woman, immediately after receiving Jesus, went back to her town and shared her personal testimony. As a result, several people went to meet Jesus and believed the good news for themselves. *"Many of the Samaritans of that city believed on Him, for the saying of the woman, which testified"* (John 4:39). We are the women who also encountered Jesus for ourselves, accepted the invitation, and brought our stories of transformation to the table. We are the women representing the *13 Seats*, who dared to testify so that others may also believe and receive.

Today King Jesus still seeks for others like us, the Samaritan woman, and Seth upon whom to bestow His kindness. In this book, He searches hearts, looking for anyone willing to respond to His beckoning of transforming love. The King has searched and has found you. Will you accept the invitation? Will you dare to testify? Arise now and go into all the world and share.

This is not the end. It is just the beginning.

For Personal Reflection

Table Talk Discussions

SEAT 1

My Journey: The Drive Home by Jackie E. Nugent

1. Jackie's story describes her risky encounters as a youth experiencing homelessness, delinquent tendencies, and teenage pregnancy. Have you or someone you know experienced a similar lifestyle? Describe your understanding of the situation. Consider the perspectives of: youth, parents, community, and environment.

2. *"For the intent of man's heart is evil from his youth"* (Genesis 8:21). What is the meaning of this scripture?

3. What support or resources do you think at-risk youth may benefit from? Do you think a mentor role could have helped Jackie during this critical stage of her life, why or why not? Describe the impact of environment and peers on lifestyle choices.

4. Do you think the school counsellor should have called Jackie's parents? How significant is professional interventions? If you need professional help, how would you find it?

5. When does parenting stop? Is it when a child becomes a parent? Should parents of pregnant teens help to support with child rearing? Describe some benefits and drawbacks of assisting? Explain if there is such a thing as too much or too little when it comes to helping?

6. "One generation plants the seed, the next generation gets the shade" (Chinese Proverb). Think about the seed(s) your fore-parents planted for you (for example, morals and values). How have you benefited from the seed(s) and how have you experienced or cultivated the shade provided?

7. Luke 2:52 (NIV) describes Jesus' growth and development in the following four areas. Consider how underdevelopment in these areas can affect the process of maturity and character as an adult.

   Jesus Grew—matured, increased, and developed—in:

   - **WISDOM** – Intellectually. How important is education and continuous learning to you?

   - **STATURE** – Physically. How can more emphasis be placed on how we look after our physical health?

   - **FAVOUR** with God – Spiritually. How can your connection to your spiritual need for God be improved?

   - **FAVOUR** with man – Relationally. How are you adding value to your sphere of influence at home, at work, or in your community?

8. Read 2 Corinthians 5:17-21 & Romans 8:1. Explain how a person who may be considered a "black sheep" or who is facing an identity crisis can apply these texts to their life.

9. What words of encouragement could be shared with a young person or a parent who is struggling?

SEAT 2

Mirror Mirror by Yolando Robinson

1. Does it make you uncomfortable to look at yourself in the mirror? Why or why not?

2. Psalm 139:14 states that we have been *"fearfully and wonderfully made."* How does this scripture impact the way you see yourself? What might cause someone to doubt the truth in that verse?

3. In Yolando's chapter, we find that she did not receive the affirmation of beauty she wanted from others. Have you found this to be your experience, and how has it molded your view of yourself? How important is affirmation to you?

4. 1 Samuel 16:7 (ESV) says, *"The Lord sees not as man sees: man looks on the outward appearance, but the Lord looks on the heart."* What do you think this means? How does society shape our standards about outward appearance? Why do you think God cares more about our heart?

5. Think about someone who might be struggling with poor self-image. Imagine them sitting next to you right now. How would you testify to that person? What could you say to reassure them?

SEAT 3

A Voice from the Pew by Amber Shurr-Sloss

1. As a result of abuse, Amber believed that she was damaged goods and that her value was only in what she could do for others. What are some of the lies that you or someone who has been abused might be deceived by? Explain the implication of John 17:17 (NKJV) *"Sanctify them by Your truth. Your word is truth."*

2. When Amber tried to tell what happened to her, she was not supported. What can be done to create a safe space to hear and support the "cry" of another, and what can be done to help protect the vulnerable among us?

3. When a person in a position of authority misuses his or her power, what are some barriers and opportunities to address him or her? Who else should intervene?

4. Explain the importance of forgiveness and breaking the cycle of hurt and harm for victims and abusers.

5. Hurting people often wait for their abuser to fix the inexplicable damage caused. What does Psalm 143:7 teach us?

SEAT

His Treasure Through Grief by Narkie Assimeh

1. How do major life events, such as planning a funeral or learning of a loved one's terminal illness affect one's ability to grieve?

2. Mary Stevenson's poem "Footprints in the Sand" is an amazing illustration of God being with us even though we may not feel His presence. What are some things you can do to keep the line of communication open with our Saviour during times of grief and loss?

3. In Narkie's story, she shares about feeling joy that her mother passed in her place of birth. In the eye of grief, Narkie found the blessing. God challenges us in 1 Thessalonians 5:12 to do just that. Read the scripture and think of what blessings you can find in the midst of tremendous grief and loss?

SEAT

Grace Within the Walls by Elle Leaño

1. Elle mentions praying for her loved ones while she was trapped behind prison walls. Can you talk about how you cope with the loss of everyday contact with your loved ones? How do you stay connected to loved ones who are somehow separated from you?

2. There is a temptation to conceal our experiences. How would you keep your children from the same negative course of actions you chose?

3. We are instructed to train up our children in the way they should go; and when they are old they will not depart from it (Proverbs 22:6 KJV). What are some of the things you can do to help your child avoid certain pitfalls?

4. Do you believe in additional support services for children of incarcerated mothers? If yes, what would this look like to you? If no, how can the cycle of incarceration be prevented in the children of inmates?

5. If you had a chance to redo your life, what would you do differently? Explain.

SEAT 6

Cry of My Heart by Mirtha A. Coronel

1. What might be hindering the deepest desires you have from coming to pass? Might this be a yearning to do something greater that God has called you to do? Be encouraged, *"For God did not send his Son into the world to condemn the world, but to save the world through him"* (NIV).

2. Do you know your identity in Christ? If not, what is the cry of your heart?

3. John 4:13 (NIV) states, *"But whoever drinks the water I give him will never thirst. Indeed, the water I give him will become in him a spring of water welling up to eternal life."* Ever since Mirtha drank from this living water, she has never thirsted again. Have you partaken of this living water? Have you felt a desire to taste something more than what you have been tasting thus far?

4. Mirtha's abuse was kept silent because the person she told did not believe her. Is there a dark secret that you believe you have to take with you to the grave? This is called a spiritual stronghold, a hindrance that needs to be exposed and addressed to ensure the uninterrupted flow of your divine purpose.

5. After the inception of sexual abuse, Mirtha inherited the guilt, shame, and loss of trust— the trio. She created her own safe, but dark, place. In this place, Mirtha heeded to the lies that led to a self-destructive lifestyle, which included self-harm and suicidal ideations. How can the heavy weight of this toxic trio be lifted off the soul of persons who may be silently crying for help?

6. Describe how an attack on sexual purity may look different for different people? Consider the following concepts: sexual power, sexual promiscuity, loss of intimacy.

7. Mirtha decided to go through the process of forgiving everyone that harmed her. Have you? Why or why not? What is hindering you? She also learned to genuinely release herself. How do you see yourself?

Sacred Reflection: When you cry, your tears are bringing your healing. Your tears will saturate the dry ground of your soul. All this is preparing you to germinate the seeds of love and forgiveness of Christ.

SEAT

My Gift from God by Siobhan Bent

1. Explain how the quality of parental bonding may impact the relationship between one's children and other significant relationships.

2. Are you holding on to any negative feelings from your childhood that could be hindering you from living the purposed-filled life God has already predestined for you?

3. When we go through life's experiences, even the adverse experiences have a greater purpose. It is intended for us to share our testimony to help someone else. I challenge you to reflect on an experience you had that shifted your life's trajectory, and ask God to show you who might be assigned and waiting to hear your testimony of how you overcame.

4. In Siobhan's story, she felt she was a mistake made by her mother and father. Siobhan experienced neglect and feelings of rejection from both parents. This experience hindered her maternal and paternal bonding, resulting in isolation and social withdrawal. What impact can the lack of relational bonds have on developing healthy character and healthy connections?

5. Jeremiah 1:5 (NIV) says, *"Before I formed you in the womb I knew you, before you were born I set you apart; I appointed you as a prophet to the nations."* When Siobhan questions her qualifications, she is reminded of hope found in the text that identifies a predestined purpose on the life of Jeremiah. Siobhan uses this scripture as a reminder of her call to serve the vast community of motherhood. How have you utilized your calling to serve others, in spite of past disappointments?

SEAT

Mentally I̶n̶s̶a̶n̶e̶ Faith by Naomi C. McBean

1. Naomi's struggle with mental illness had what she called an "entry point." Fear entered her heart and imprisoned her. Describe a time when you felt fearful?

2. She also talks about feeling trapped within herself, and describes her phobia of enclosed spaces. Are you able to describe a time when you felt like you were trapped? How has this experience affected you?

3. The Bible says in 2 Timothy 1:7 (NKJV) *"For God has not given us a spirit of fear, but of power and of love and of a sound mind."* Can you explain what this means to you?

4. In today's society, there is a negative stigma attached to mental illness. Can you identify reasons for this?

5. Naomi says that she remained undiagnosed as she struggled through her illness. How would you be able to identify and help someone struggling with fear, anxiety, or depression?

6. Naomi gives us a tool to use to achieve mental stability in Romans 12:2, which says, *"Be transformed by the renewing of your mind."* Explain what this process would look like in your life.

SEAT

The Prodigal Daughter by Atisha Sanderson

1. Atisha's chapter is called The Prodigal Daughter. During her struggle with alcoholism and disobedience, she received a second chance to live. Read Luke 15:11-32, the story of the prodigal son. How does Atisha's testimony relate?

2. Does God want us to continue on the path of sin? How does God love the sinner? (Read John 3:16).

3. Describe what repentance looks like for you (Read Psalm 51).

4. Read Isaiah 61:3 (NKJV). The text describes Jesus, our Saviour, and how He comforts the hurting. Fill in the blanks and practice memorizing this passage.

   a. To console those who _____ in Zion,

   b. To give them _____ for ashes,

   c. The oil of _____ for mourning,

   d. The garment of praise for the spirit of _____;

   e. That they may be called trees of _____,

   f. The planting of the Lord, that He may be _____,

Answers: a. mourn b. beauty c. joy d. heaviness e .righteousness f. glorified

SEAT 10

From Poverty to Riches by Bernice Moreau

1. Dr. Bernice describes poverty as being more than a lack of money, but also a lack of social, emotional, psychological, spiritual, and mental stability. Based on this description, can you identify areas of poverty in your own life and how they have affected you today?

2. She also talks about being considered a bad omen for her family and being blamed for the death and misfortunes of her family. Can you describe a time when you were either blamed for something you had no control over or experienced exclusion?

3. Dr. Bernice had two significant people in her life that came alongside her and mentored her. What are some ways in which you can help others who may be experiencing exclusion or abuse?

4. The Bible says in Philippians 4:19 *"God will supply all your needs according to His riches in glory in Christ Jesus."* How would you interpret this verse?

5. When Dr. Bernice talks about riches, she does not define it as silver and gold. Instead, she says that she is rich in Christ. What do you think she means by her statement?

SEAT 11

When Disability Challenges Faith by Susan Stewart

1. How can systemic barriers be addressed for people with disabilities?

2. Leviticus 19:14 reads, *"Do not curse the deaf or put a stumbling block in front of the blind, but fear your God. I am the Lord."* What does inclusion in a faith community look like?

3. How can persons with disabilities be better served or engaged in the body of Christ? What might a congregational care committee do for individuals and families living with a disability?

4. How can the body of Christ be better equipped and educated about disability? What would that education look like for a congregation?

5. In Exodus 4:10, Moses said to the Lord, *"Pardon your servant, Lord. I have never been eloquent, neither in the past nor since you have spoken to your servant. I am slow of speech and tongue."* Here Moses describes his inability.

o   What are the things you're not very good at, but you aspire to be?

o   How does this inability impact how you interact with yourself and others?

o   Moses' brother Aaron spoke for him. Describe your personal limitations and how you compensate?

Prayer: God, help me to notice what barriers exist around me, so that I can help those who need it. Lord, teach me to love people who are different from me. Amen.

SEAT

Journey to Him by Lorena Williams

1. Lorena talks about "looking for love in all the wrong places." If you were to be completely transparent, would you say that you have done the same thing? Where has that experience led you?

2. There is a growing population of children without active fathers in today's society. Lorena desired to live with the father of her child at home as a family. Do you think having a father in the home is important? Why or why not?

3. Lorena shared that at a point in her marriage her husband became her god. Can trying to please your partner with all your heart become idolatry? Explain.

4. How can you identify when a relationship is toxic?

5. Ephesians 5:22 says, *"Wives, submit to your own husbands, as to the Lord."* What do you think this means?

6. Lorena talks about her journey to God. Do you believe that marriage is an expression of God's love for us and each other?

7. How can this chapter help bring healing and restoration to marriages?

Meet the authors.

❦

From left to right—Front row: Mirtha A. Coronel, Jackie E. Nugent, Lorena Williams. Middle row: Yolando Robinson, Narkie Assimeh, Bernice Moreau, Susan Stewart, Siobhan Bent. Back row: Atisha Sanderson, Naomi C. McBean, Amber Shurr-Sloss, Elle Leaño